W9-AYB-355

AMERICAN YESTERDAY

by

Eric Sloane

DOVER PUBLICATIONS, INC.
Mineola, New York

Copyright

Copyright © 1956 by Wilfred Funk, Inc.
Copyright © Renewed 1984 by Eric Sloane
All rights reserved.

Bibliographical Note

This Dover edition, first published in 2003, is an unabridged republication of the work originally published in 1956 by Funk & Wagnalls, New York.

Library of Congress Cataloging-in-Publication Data

Sloane, Eric.
    American yesterday / Eric Sloane.
        p. cm.
    ISBN 0-486-42760-9 (pbk.)
    1. United States—Social life and customs—1783-1865. 2. Architecture—United States—History—19th century. 3. Occupations—United States—History—19th century. I. Title.

E161.S58 2003
973.5—dc21

                                                                    2002041560

Manufactured in the United States of America
Dover Publications, Inc., 31 East 2nd Street, Mineola, N.Y. 11501

Author's Note

THIS IS A BOOK about our national attic of vanishing ways and obsolete occupations. As always, when sorting through things of the past, we have an uncontrollable urge to save that which we believe to be good and to discard that which we regard as undesirable. Too often, the apparently worthless later reveals its true value.

In observing some of our collections of Americana, a child might picture America's past as a strange world of hand-made artifacts in the possession of people who spent half their lives creating them and the other half living with them. I have collected many of the wondrous things which great-grandfather made, but I have always felt that the old gentleman himself was slighted. If only some of his ways of life might be preserved or his thoughts better recorded, my collection would then be more complete. I am sure that I would prefer that my descendants find in my life a graciousness worthy of perpetuation than simply to decorate their houses with the obsolete implements of my everyday life and regard them only as quaint curiosities.

The antique things and wooden oddities that give me such pleasure ao open glorious doors to the past; yet, if I could only meet and speak with the men who made them, an important hunger would be satisfied. The *living* difference or lack of difference between us and our ancestors is a revealing thing; this, and not the change in our attic material, is the proof of progress.

This book is dedicated to those who have kept the past alive, rescuing and sorting discarded objects with fond hands, yet not always knowing exactly why they were doing so; to those who hold to the New England belief that everything comes to good use in time, if one has the patience to wait.

May these pages stir new and urgent voices of ghosts among your relics. May you listen and hear the living heritage of America, and, most urgent of all, may you decorate and enrich your everyday life with it.

ERIC SLOANE

New Milford, Conn.
July, 1956

How Different was Great-grandfather?

IT IS ODD what profound thoughts can come to mind when one is not consciously trying to think. There certainly exists no invitation to contemplation while doing sixty miles an hour on a highway or rumbling to work on a noisy morning train, yet some of our deepest thoughts seem to occur at such times. Perhaps it is an American way of thinking, setting us off from the rest of the world. Instead of meditating while resting, as Europeans do, we seem to labor just as hard at our relaxation and often meditate best when we work the hardest. Like our forefathers who created a pattern for a new world while simultaneously splitting rails, building stone walls, and fighting off Indians, many Americans still do much of their thinking while they are busiest.

It seems natural, then, that the thought which prompted this writing should have occurred during a hurried automobile journey to the city. Observing the rush of traffic over highways which only a few years ago were desolate pastures, I found my mind dwelling on the effects of such progress. Exactly what, I wondered, have been the actual effects of this last century on the American man?

We are supposed to be healthier, wealthier, and living in better times. Few of us would argue with that contention. But is the man at the wheel of today's automobile essentially the same man who drove a surrey a century ago? Is he the same kind of man merely wearing different clothes and doing different things, or has he actually undergone a physical and mental and spiritual change? If there is some change, no matter how small, it seems worthy of study. It could be one of the important observations of our time.

9

How much of the American legend have we inherited? One cannot help feeling that there were giants of men walking our land a century or two ago. Yet the crude countryside that gave us our first statesmen should in its present "improved state" produce even greater men. We unconsciously picture ourselves in the image of the early American without realizing that his descendants are subject to change.

We have made a national cliché of the "American way," which unfortunately has in so many minds become synonymous with capitalism. But the American way is no recent industrial-age invention. It flourished as vigorously perhaps, or more so, in the early days when most of our needs were satisfied through barter and money was a strange giant just invading the scene. If the American has altered during that period, or if we have created a different national philosophy, we should certainly be the first to realize it. Changing industrial eras are as normal as new-model automobiles, but a shift in the attitude toward life is a symptom to be watched.

There are those who cannot conceive that a single century can exert a noticeable effect on mankind. If it were impossible, however, there still would be no reason for not discussing the impossibility. However, time and change have already affected plant and animal life. The quality of our average landscape can be scientifically proven to have been altered from that of a century ago through erosion and exhaustion. The rich earth and moss and the first-growth trees that sprang from it have changed to a poorer soil and a different grade of wood. Man may well have changed to a lesser or greater degree.

.. One Century

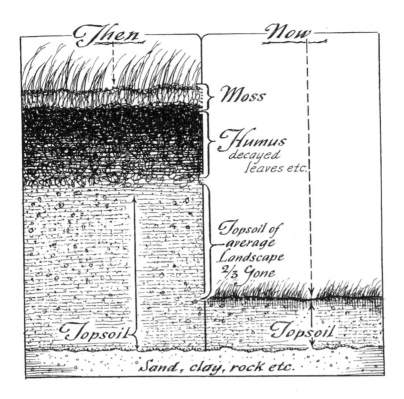

It is easier, however, to analyze a physical alteration in a nation's soil and wood than it is to isolate a less tangible change in its people. In analyzing great-grandfather scientifically, we would have to take into account such physical elements as heat and moisture, gases, dust, noise, and the various other environmental factors that make modern life different from that of the past. We would have to compare changes in manual labor, habits of sleep, and the character of food. These things exert their effect upon people and all these conditions have altered during this one century.

It has almost been forgotten, for example, that the world in which we move about today is much drier. The early American farmer invariably wore boots because he continually walked on moist ground. Even the village worker lived in a wet world because all factories were mills built over water-power. The consequence of two centuries of reclaiming wet lands and building cities on the sites of former marshes and meadows has been the creation of a far different workaday climate.

Despite this distinct climatic alteration, the weather during the last hundred years has not changed as much as the landscape has. The virgin forest and mossy topsoil of a century ago were a natural sponge, absorbing rains which now roll across the surface of "tired," dry landscapes and into abnormally swollen rivers. A New England farmer put it nicely by comparing today's landscape with a modern blotter. "It used to be," he said, "that blotters were just made for absorbing ink. Now they are money-makers with one whole side advertising some darned thing instead of doing the job they were intended to do. That's the way the whole countryside is getting. Bulldozers are covering over the good bog-meadows with money-making real-estate developments. When a good rain comes, it runs over the top of the ground, just like ink on the wrong side of a blotter."

Boots for the wet world of yesterday

A century ago, towering first-growth trees broke raindrops into tiny particles, turning a large portion of rainfall back into the atmosphere by evaporation before it reached the ground. The trees' great roots braced the soil and made a framework for moss and peat that held as much as ten to fifteen times its weight in water. The farmer, who never ventured outdoors without his traditional boots, accepted moisture more contentedly than does the man of today. The swimming hole, the pond, the creek and ditch and bog-meadow were a necessary adjunct to his farmland operations. Now they are regarded as nuisances of nature to be filled in and "improved." Such are the changes that have come to the average American landscape in a century.

According to collectors of early American clothing, it is evident that over this period the average American woman has grown taller and the man a bit shorter. An estimated ten million American men sit their way through life, either at meals, coffee-breaks, at the office, in automobiles, before the TV, or at the baseball stadium; the average American male's waistline has changed accordingly. A hundred years ago, the American would have done an average day's work as morning chores before starting his actual occupation. The few people who now walk to work or to the morning train are regarded as physical culturists. According to reliable research, American men live so much in a sitting or "relaxed" position that they use up less than half the calories they did seventy-five years ago. To illustrate how rapidly changes in the human body can evolve, consider the findings of Dr. Wilson T. Sowder in *The Journal of Lifetime Living,* who agrees that American men are becoming physically inferior to their women. In 1920, the mortality rate of white men between 45 and 54 was already ten per cent higher than that of women; in 1950, it was seventy-eight per cent higher! The outdoor clubs, to which the average business man belonged seventy-five years ago, have vanished. Bicycling and hiking are now "for Boy Scouts." It seems that America's most disastrous invention may be, not the atomic bomb, but the easy chair.

In another hundred years, barring war or pestilence, there will be seven billion people on this earth, or about three times as many as now exist. The land will be proportionately that much more worn out, and its mineral content that much more depleted. Irrigating the deserts and de-salting the sea water will enable farming to feed the seven billion, but how different will be the average American's life and diet from those of the first settlers! In the refined diet of the present day, about two-thirds of our calories are supplied from food which has been stripped of nutrients. A few generations ago, the very poor were deriving more nutritive value from their food than do the very rich today.

It is important to remember, when comparing the past with the present, not to allow modern wonders to awe one into believing that all changes are synonymous with progress. "The old way" is not necessarily an inefficient way. William Morris said, "The great achievement of the nineteenth century was the making of machines which were the wonders of invention, skill, and patience and which were used for the production of measureless quantities of worthless make-shifts." However rash this statement may appear, the more one analyzes it, the more truth one will discover in it.

It is difficult, perhaps impossible, for anyone to believe that progress and improvement may be accompanied by inconvenience or danger. Nevertheless, consider the average modern electrified house. If the current went off for a week during the winter, the oil furnace would fail to operate, water pumps would stop, lights would go out, cooking would cease, and the plumbing might burst. The house would be rendered unlivable unless it also contained an old-fashioned fireplace, a cook-stove, and candles or kerosene lights. Consider a modern metropolis such as New York City. If it were completely shut off from outside territory, its food supplies would last only a matter of days, and starvation would overcome its population perhaps in one or two months. The ancient farmhouse, without plumbing but with a large woodpile and its own source of food, gave its owner a better sense of security than we might suppose. The smallest village with its own water-powered mills was actually more self-sufficient than the average metropolis of today! Progress and speed become more treacherous as they increase.

An early London newspaper once criticized us for our haste. "Speed kills five hundred people a day in America," it said. A New England paper retaliated good-naturedly, but with a great deal of truth, "It isn't the speed that kills us, you know, it's the quick stop." And so in modern everyday living, the pace is often of less importance than is the dilemma of having to stop.

Great-grandfather did things always with a purpose. He did them conscientiously because he did them himself. That is why he so often put his name and the date on his belongings. Today we might do the same thing for sentiment, but the dates one sees on old things were put there in pride, as if to say, "In this year I was satisfied with this piece of work which I myself created."

The awareness of life and time which seemed to permeate the early days shone brightest in the home. When a man built his house, he might not put his name upon it, but the date seemed all-important. His position in the stream of time and a consciousness of the part he was playing were part of a rare experience that few of us are now privileged to enjoy.

Often there was special sentiment connected with a date such as "E.A.C., 1781" carved in a topmost rafter of a house built by Ebenezer Clark and his wife Abigail, near Washington, Connecticut. Whenever they built substantial houses, the Germans in Pennsylvania made date-stones which not only incorporated the owner's name but included a blessing on the house. A typical inscription upon a 1771 date-stone reads, "To Thy care, O Lord, are commended all in this household going in or out."

14

Dates were often mosaicked into brick walls. They were put into fireplace backs, twisted into the anchoring irons of brick sidewalls, carved into some main beam of the house, and even designed into the over-all pattern of

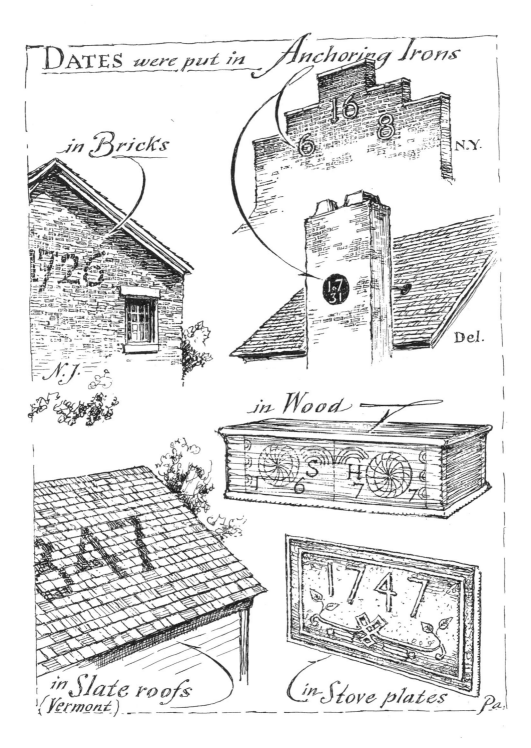

DATES *were put in* Anchoring Irons

in Bricks

16 8
6

N.Y.

17 31

Del.

1726

N.J.

in Wood

S H
1 6 7 7

in Slate roofs
(Vermont)

1747

(in Stove plates

Pa.

NAMES were put on Tools.

German felling Ax 1800

GUTH

Broadax
R.I., 1817

FELDE
1817

. . . . on Boxes
and Chests . . .

Jn. HUBER his hand

Sarah Hopts

EBENEZER T

and Barns . . .

H. SCHULZE

and any creation of which the maker was proud

slate roofs. It is always obvious that they were put there for others to see in some distant future. The old-timers firmly believed that those who fail to look backward at their ancestors seldom look ahead to posterity. The pioneer looked both ways in those days, and the knowledge of his own relative position created a gratifying American philosophy of content.

It is a pity that a man's work should outlive his identity, yet many of the old barns and farmhouses had identifying information which was obliterated when it became the vogue to "preserve wood with paint." The better timber of those days did not, of course, require a preservative coat, and the oldest surviving wooden structures are still the unpainted ones. Paint eventually has a decaying effect on moist wood; unless it is kept in constant repair, soft wood actually seasons better without it. In addition to this scientific reason for keeping wood bare, for a long while it was considered vulgar to paint one's house. The red barn of New England is comparatively recent. Not until Pennsylvania barns had sported paint, fancy weathervanes, and decorative designs for almost a century did the conservative New Englander dare to alter the appearance of the naked seasoned wood of his farm buildings. But the paint era evolved suddenly and barns with names and dates upon them soon lost that valuable information under many coats of paint during the years which followed. There is now hardly a barn with positive identification left in America.

The early American's urge for identification was born of pride, both in himself and in his time; but we are now so taken up with progress and money-making that identifying ourselves and our time has become almost meaning-less. For example, you will not find a date on any part of your automobile. Its year, which represents nothing but depreciation, can be found only hidden away in a used-car price book. Trade names are on everything about the home, but the name of the designer and the date on which it was made can scarcely be found.

It is interesting to note that things made nowadays with "do-it-yourself" kits are almost always identified by the maker's name and date. Only a few do-it-yourselfers make their own things to save money; it is the thrill of recapturing that lost satisfaction of creativeness that really makes it worthwhile. At the turn of the century, when "do-it-yourself" kits were sold to burn pictures already traced into leather postcards, *Harper's Weekly* predicted that "such mechanized art will sound the death-knell for the creative urge of our young artists." Today's painting kits, with numbered colors and pictures outlined ready to fill in, would really insult great-grandfather. He had no inferiority complex about creating, and he conceived all sorts of original and primitive designs, just as did his wife with quilts and his daughter with samplers.

17

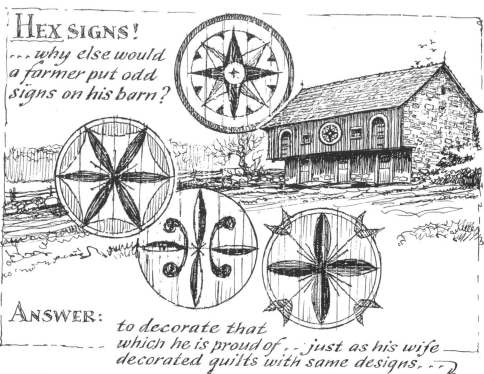

HEX SIGNS!

...why else would a farmer put odd signs on his barn?

ANSWER:

to decorate that which he is proud of ... just as his wife decorated quilts with same designs...

Great-grandfather enjoyed the proud life of an artist living among artists; everything about him he had created himself. He made farms out of forests and he built his house with tools fashioned by his own hands. In simply living his own life, he was creating villages and towns. But, alas, everything we touch nowadays has been created by others. We have been robbed of our creativeness and the result is often a moral emptiness. Yet, like unemployed actors who continue to live in the glory of their pasts, modern men will never give up the dream of returning to that wonderful world of great-grandfather. Meanwhile, most of us must be content to be the healthiest and wealthiest audience to mechanical greatness in all history.

Only a few years ago everyone carried a folding knife called a penknife. Many men still carry penknives, yet few know that they are so called because they were designed for sharpening crow quills before the time of steel pens. Aged men enjoyed whittling with their penknives, but nowadays you will seldom see anyone whittling. It was a joy to keep a knife sharp and clean, just as it was to keep an ax in perfect condition. Creativeness need not always be a thing of splendor: there is sufficient beauty in a pile of well-stacked kindling or a clean-cut pile of cordwood to make a man feel good. The satisfaction of seeing rich pine split into sweet-smelling sections of kindling was only a small part of life's pleasures, but it was also a part of boyhood training that a man enjoyed remembering.

...even the wood-pile is a Creation on the farm.

19

Our dilemma of emptiness lies in no lack of ability; it lies rather in a lack of understanding. We are led to believe, for instance, that to be creative we must be original. The early American artist naturally adopted classic and ancient design wherever he could. His architectural ability lay in understanding and recognizing the best things of the past and in making use of them, *not in being an inventor*. His special genius was more often his ability to refrain from being original! He preserved the good art of the past by incorporating it in everything he built; but our idea of preservation has sadly changed. Now we preserve buildings of *historic interest,* with only secondary consideration of their design. We save things of the past by putting a proud date upon them so that they become poor servants of nostalgia. A sense of history thus becomes a national apology wherever a sense of beauty is lacking.

If you were to define briefly the difference between the man of today and the man of the past you might find the word "awareness" very descriptive. Fiorello LaGuardia, in praising air transportation, said that he dozed into slumber in a plane at Chicago and landed in New York without being aware of having left the ground. A century ago you would have been conscious of every mile of travel, counted by the bumps and turns and stops and starts. Uncomfortable, indeed, but you would have been awake to the experience of the trip. One of the wonders of jet-plane travel lies in the fact that there is no sensation of movement and the passenger remains unaware of speed. We have relegated the inconvenience of travel to the past, but we have also lost our wonderful awareness of the experience.

A cross-country trip, an air flight, or a sea voyage once called for much thought and some strength, but things are made easier now. The day of great pilots has passed because the need for great pilots no longer exists. A push-button flight to the moon will some day become boresome, but the Davey Crocketts and Wyatt Earps and the Lindberghs will always excite the American mind.

A jet-plane test pilot was asked to recount his greatest thrill in flying. His reply is interesting. "Years ago in an air circus," he said, "I flew an old Curtiss-Wright pusher as a stunt. It wasn't the danger of flying an old crate that gave me the thrill; it was being out in the open with wires whistling all around, the way the first flyers did, feeling each updraft and flying almost as birds do. I did only about thirty miles an hour, but I still make that flight in my dreams."

The antique automobile fans who go on trips in their obsolete cars are not exhibitionists. In fact, they would happily dispense with spectators. They are enjoying a slice of the past and the unique experience of making a trip in one age, with an awareness that belongs to another.

Great-grandfather was intensely awake to everything about him. He knew where his clothes came from, because the cloth was made in his own home. All the things in his house were more than familiar to him: he had made them himself. Today the average city person has not the slightest idea where his tap water or heat or light and power or food come from. He knows only the location of faucets and switches; he takes the rest for granted. He cannot conceive that he might derive some satisfaction from knowing where these conveniences originate; to him, the most important thing is the ability to pay for them. The satisfaction of being completely aware of all that goes on around us has become a lost art.

It is typical of America today to say, "If I only knew *then* what I know *today*," or "I certainly didn't appreciate what I had," or "I didn't know when I was well off." Such afterthoughts are the result of having lived without a full consciousness of life. We are often in such a hurry to get somewhere that we don't care too much where somewhere is. As long as we are working and on our way, we are morally and economically content.

Satisfaction with one's lot was to great-grandfather something to be learned while very young and remembered for the rest of one's life. But it has now become an American virtue to be dissatisfied! It is acknowledged that dissatisfaction results in improvement or the invention of something new; that is good. But satisfaction has its benefits, too, and should least of all be ignored. When you accept dissatisfaction as a virtue, you trade in your good automobile when the lines are slightly out of style, or anything else that becomes "dated," in spite of its continuing efficiency.

Progress has become so involved with dissatisfaction that modern salesmanship and advertising depend largely upon instilling discontent with what one already possesses. Any given product is advertised one year as "what you should be satisfied with" and advertised the year following as "what you should be dissatisfied with." It is now regarded an insult to a person to say that he is "easily satisfied!"

It might not be considered progressive to be satisfied with last year's model, but it is certainly a worthwhile adventure in contentment.

a Dissatisfied American, 1902 style.

Great-grandfather's Church.

"THANK GOD," say the antiquarians, "the church is one thing which hasn't changed." But great-grandfather would be saddened at some of our new church buildings, particularly those which have been built in the so-called progressive style of modern architecture. There is a brave school of thought among designers which holds that man should try not to look backward, even if the view is pleasant. If a church can be made to appear to be farthest away from what all other churches have ever resembled, we are supposed to have reached a goal, especially when we have created a church which resembles nothing ever built before in this architectural form.

The church, of course, is not the only architecture attacked by "progressive creativeness." The average filling station, deprived of tanks and signs, could often pass for a modern home; many of our apartment buildings resemble penitentiaries; some banks might double for automobile show rooms, and dog hospitals for inns.

Two hundred years ago, when twenty men built their homes in one group, there was a common source of inspiration; although each house was individual, they all were traditionally correct and they blended into one pleasing composition. Twenty men given free reign to build their dream houses today would produce twenty more efficient buildings, but a revolting group of architectural contrasts. On the other hand, when a modern development is planned for one particular style, the result usually looks like something from a mechanical production line.

23

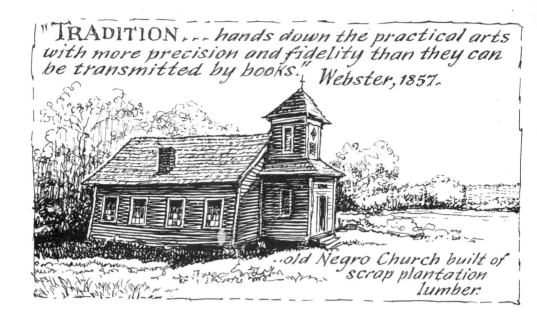

"TRADITION .... *hands down the practical arts with more precision and fidelity than they can be transmitted by books.*" Webster, 1857.

...old Negro Church built of scrap plantation lumber.

During the past few years many roadside shopping centers have grown into villages. "They become a village," real-estate developers say, "when a bank building joins the group." It used to be the rule that the church was the center of the village, with homes and shops spreading outward from it. Ironically enough in this age, if great-grandfather were seeking the village center, he would be directed to the bank building instead of the church.

Great-grandfather did not go to church simply because he enjoyed the service; he enjoyed discipline and he was aware of its benefits. The appreciation of discipline seems to be another vanished grace; the actual meaning of the word has even changed within one century. Webster defines it as: "obsolete) teaching, instruction"; the other and more modern definition is: "punishment, chastisement." Discipline was originally an ecclesiastical word, derived from the word "disciple," and it referred to a set of rules for good conduct with no reference to punishment. The newer use of the word discipline and the American interpretation of freedom clash, so in that round-about way discipline itself has become a distasteful thing to many of us in the present day.

Freedom without discipline in the old sense of the word was deplored by the old-timers. Alexis Carrel said: "Emancipated man is by no means comparable to an eagle soaring in the sky. He far more closely resembles a dog escaped from its kennel and dashing hither and thither among the traffic. He can indeed, like a dog, do exactly as he pleases and go wherever he wants. He is

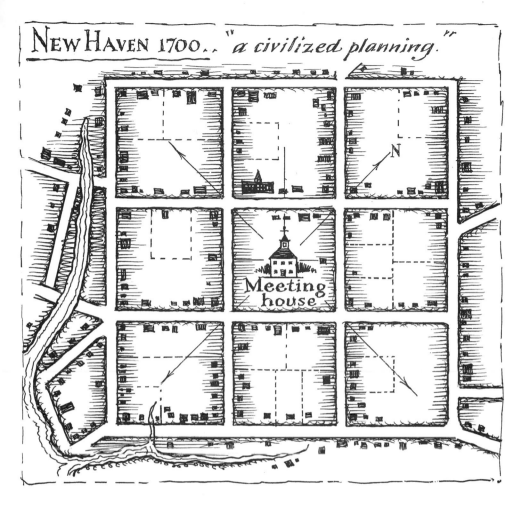

NEW HAVEN 1700... "a civilized planning."

Meeting house

none the less lost because he does not know where to go or how to protect himself from the dangers which surround him. How is he to discover once again the moral security his ancestors knew when they built the Gothic cathedrals?" A telling point, indeed, for old-time religion!

Psychiatrists explain that people who dwell in the past are escaping from a present with which they are not content. Perhaps that simplification explains why so many of us find it pleasing and comfortable to decorate modernistic houses with bits of early Americana, often incongruous in the surrounding décor. Even more interesting is the possibility that many antiquarians are escaping from religious insecurity because in their ability to "dwell in the past" they are automatically assuring themselves of a hereafter!

The idea is not new. The preface to the *Connecticut Historical Collections* of 1830 begins: "The power by which we recall past scenes, the rapidity with which they are brought in review before us, the faculty by which we can range o'er creation, and dwell upon the past and future, demonstrates that man was indeed formed in the image of his Creator, and destined for immortality. By the contemplation of the past, we feel our span of existence extended: we enter into the thoughts, hopes, and aspirations of generations before us, and in such moments hold communion with the departed spirits of antiquity."

Escaping the present to recapture the past's religious security may be inconvenient, but it is not at all unhealthy. If there is any truth to the belief that some antiquarians cling to the past for such a psychological reason, there is still no cause for regret. Once the truth were known to them, they would suddenly find themselves collecting art, whereas previously they were collecting only historical curiosities of the past. They might, for the first time, see in a room in which Washington slept the beauty that was previously overshadowed by the picture of a great man asleep there.

The Christmas-card interpretation of early churchgoers has never been a true picture. Very often, for example, the familiar tall steeple was added years later, after bells were cast on this side of the sea. The first church was

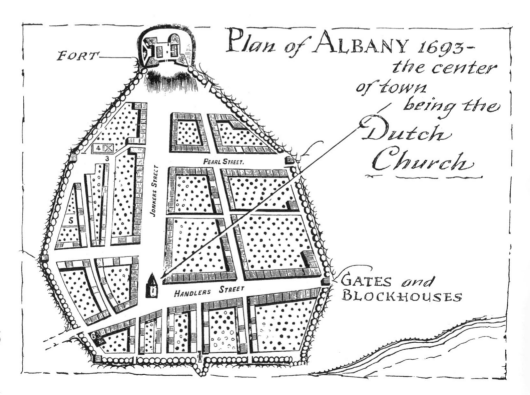

26

Foot Stoves. *You brought your own heat!*

1650

1750

called a meeting house and it resembled exactly that. It was used for all sorts of town meetings during the week and it became a church only at sundown on Saturday, when the Sabbath started, and lasted until sundown on Sunday. Sunday night was not the quiet eve that it is today, for as soon as sundown occurred, fasting ended and the partying began. Because no cooking or other utilitarian work was allowed during the Sabbath, mother labored all day Saturday, but stopped at the moment the sun dropped below the horizon.

Churches were unheated primarily because of the dread of accidental fire. There were no chimneys, as you may have noticed in pictures of the early church buildings. In any event, an open fire built in a large building that had been closed overnight during winter would do little more than thaw the walls out.

Church services used to start at nine in the morning and lasted until dusk because by town vote no lights were allowed in most early American churches. The first lights in church buildings appeared about 1820. The first stoves were installed at about the same time, but against much protest. Churches were the coldest houses in town during the early days, and many a preacher's winter diary included such a phrase as "bread was frozen at the Lord's Table today." Bread used in celebration of the Lord's Supper was kept in a charcoal heater in most Maine churches to keep it from freezing. Baptismal water was kept under the parson's coat in a warm flask.

27

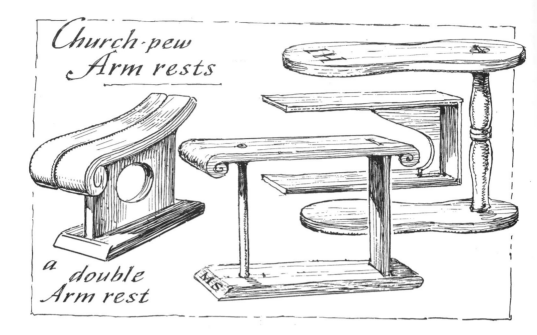

Church-pew Arm rests

a double Arm rest

The fact that children were taken to church to be baptized the Sunday following their birth, even in winter, is typical of early religion. If the church happened to be nearby, it would be bad enough, but there were often long rides by sled to the unheated church, which sometimes actually caused the child to "die of baptism." On January 22nd, 1694, Judge Sewall wrote, "A very extraordinary Storm by reason of the falling and driving of the Snow. Few women could get to Meeting. A child named Alexander was baptized in the afternoon." He did not, however, record Alexander's death a week later.

The "hardest seats in the world" were church seats. Cushions were frowned on as improper for use in church, and some of the early carpenters found play for their sense of humor by billing for "church planks of ye softest pine for comfort." Arm rests eliminated some discomfort during the tedious all-day services, but few churches supplied them. There are still many wooden arm rests with names carved upon them, indicating that owners often left their arm rests in the pews rather than carry them between home and church. There must have been many things taken to church, what with foot-warmers, pillows, blankets, arm rests, often spittoons and other conveniences. One church built in 1843 by the whaling men of Sag Harbor, Long Island, was equipped with a brass spittoon in each of its mahogany-trimmed pews.

It is strange to think of the early preacher giving his sermon with greatcoat and ear muffs on and a muffler over his head, yet this is precisely what he did during winter. When he pointed heavenward, it was often with a mittened hand, or with a hand that was immediately afterward plunged into a fur wrapper. House stoves were, for some strange reason, considered sacrilegious in a house of God, but one Vermont pastor made a giant foot stove upon which he stood all the while he preached. House stoves finally had to be voted on, and one of Connecticut's finest anecdotes involves two old maids who were opposed to a stove in their church. They were outvoted by the rest of the parish, however, and *two* big stoves were installed. One autumn day, after fanning themselves vigorously and complaining loudly about the overheated room, the ladies fainted from the "unnatural heat." But the stoves, they learned after being revived, were not even lit!

A description of the early American church worth remembering was given by the pastor of Longmeadow Church in Massachusetts almost a century ago:

"It is the Sabbath Day; the second bell, first peal. The population comes from all angles, on foot, in carriages, in farm wagons without springs. Some are drawn by horses, some by oxen. Women and younger children and older men sit on straight-backed chairs and milking stools set on the green; young men and maidens, and the boys, line the wayside, talking in whispers. Having walked all the way barefoot to keep their shoes shiny (and save them from wear, too), boys and girls are now putting shoes on and buttoning them.

"This day belongs to the church and nothing is done aside from that. No wagon or stage-coach or man afoot is moving except in accordance with the Lord's Day. Bridge and highway tolls are forbidden. New England statutes as late as a century ago put a twenty-dollar fine on any 'driver or proprietor of any coach, wagon, or sleigh upon the highway on the Lord's Day, except for necessity or charity.' "

The bell begins to toll and the congregation throngs the meeting-house steps. It is the day of greetings, the social exchange, the news day. Dr. Williams emerges from the parsonage in gown and bands and powdered wig, three-cornered hat, knee breeches, woolen stockings, and silver shoe buckles. The bell will not stop tolling until he passes through the double door and goes into the high pulpit under the great sounding board. The deacons are seated in their railed pew beneath the pulpit.

There is no stove. For fifty-one years the frosty air of the new meeting house was mitigated only by the women's foot stoves and the cracking together of frozen boot heels. The parson sometimes preached in a heavy homespun cloak; at the nooning, grateful indeed was the roaring fire in the great kitchen of the parsonage, at the tavern barroom, at all the hospitable neighbors' open houses.

The congregation stands up to pray—bodily infirmity alone prevents. If one sits down in prayer time, it is a sudden and emphatic protest against the parson's praying for the king and royal family—not that he is a Tory or inimical to the liberties of America, only an old man to whom the times look dark and fears are in the way. In due time he reads from the pulpit, though not without some misgivings, the Declaration of Independence.

For fifty years the congregation sat down to sing; but after the pitch pipe no longer toots, and the singing master has organized the choir, and the bass viols and flutes conspire with young men and maidens to make a joyful noise, they now rise up and face about to see the choir.

The gallery of the meeting house runs around the east, south, and west; square pews line the gallery walls. The Negro pew is in the southwest corner; the boys of twelve occupy the next pew, the boys of fourteen the next, those of eighteen the next (it having the advantage of a window), and the boys of sixteen the last pew on that side. A similar arrangement for the girls obtains in the eastern gallery; the single men and women of discreet age occupy the pews lining the south gallery wall. The choir seats run all around the gallery front, and the smaller children sit on benches directly behind the choir. In such an arrangement, the necessity for tithing-men is great. The seats of honor are in the broad aisle pews, below and nearest the pulpit. The pews are all free, but the seating committee assigns them. They are first instructed to wait on Dr. Williams and to know his pleasure, what pew he chooses his family to sit in. But, after that, "dignifying the house" is no easy task. Age is one consideration, property another, standing yet another.

The vanished customs of the early American church could fill a lengthy book. Because the church was the center of all village life, it seems odd that its ways have changed as much as they have. The church bell, for example, was once a sort of town crier; it spoke to tell of births and deaths, of fire and war. After a death, the bell greeted the morning with "three times three for a man, and three times two for a woman." Then after a short silence, the bell pealed out the number of years the dead person had lived. All church bells rang three times a day, at seven o'clock in the morning, at noon, and at nine o'clock for curfew. Striking each hour is a recent custom. At evening, the last ringing was followed by strokes indicating the day of the month, a signal for many a farmer to turn to his farm diary and complete the day's entry.

The tone and range of its church bell was the talk and pride of every village. The ways of the weather were often sensed by the sound of the bell. Any old-timer could tell you which way the wind was blowing, whether the barometric pressure was up or down, and what tomorrow's weather was going to be by the church bell's muffled hollowness or its crisp clarity. When one of the

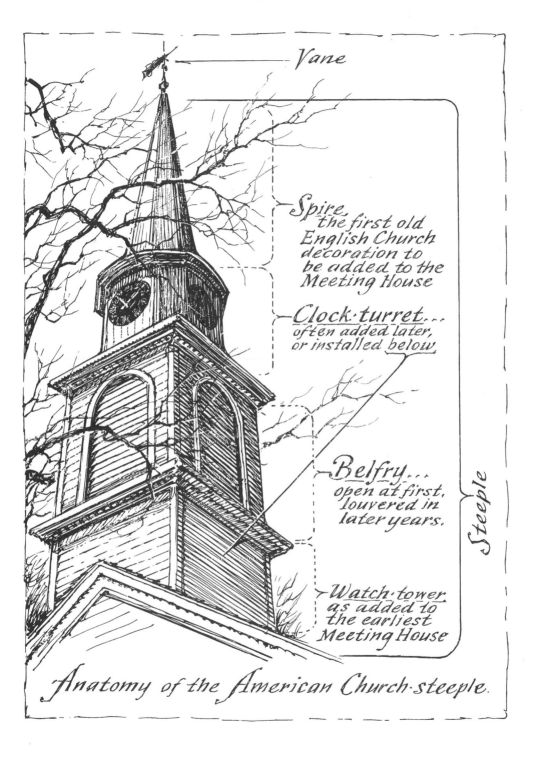

Vane

Spire, the first old English Church decoration to be added to the Meeting House

Clock·turret... often added later, or installed below.

Belfry... open at first, louvered in later years.

Watch·tower as added to the earliest Meeting House

Steeple

Anatomy of the American Church·steeple.

better-known early bells cracked and was recast with silver from donations of coins, the parson told everyone that the good act had added a special quality to the bell's tone. From that time on, cracked bells were usually recast with donated silver "to make ye tone clearer." During the Kennebunk fire of 1824, the town's church bell was heard clearly in Alfred, Maine, eleven miles away. The limit of thunder's carrying power is supposed to be ten miles, so the Kennebunk bell had set a record! It was called the only bell "louder than thunder."

Collecting taxes was a full-time job yesterday, and the tithing-man had a varied set of jobs to contend with, even during the Sabbath. There were special fines to collect from people who left their dogs unleashed during the summer Sabbath; dogs often followed their masters into the church, where a dog fight might upset the quiet of the proceedings. There were fines for those who left burning coals behind in their foot-warmers after the services. The tithing-man was always given a convenient place in the first American churches, and it was his job to keep order. His badge was a long stick with a rabbit's foot on one end and a fox tail on the other. The heavy end of the stick was used to waken nodding boys; the faces of slumbering matrons were brushed with the softer end. This was always good for a laugh, but undue noise was reprimanded by the tithing-man's holding a forefinger across his lips and tapping his stick with the other hand. The "finger-to-the-lips" sign for quiet may well have originated from the church and the tithing-man.

At first, there were square pews, sometimes curtained off to keep the draft out and to keep body heat in. Bearskins, carpets, and blankets were brought into the pews, and foot stoves were kept fed with coals from "Sabbath Day Houses" nearby. Sabbath Day houses or Sabbaday houses, as they were more often called, were little buildings put up at a respectful distance from the church and equipped with stools and blankets. Fireplaces were built in the center. A caretaker or servant was left in charge to keep the fires going and

Tithing-man's Church-stick

Children   *Adults*

a Connecticut 1760
Sabbaday House

bed   bed

Men   Women

coals were continually carried into the church pews to replenish the footstoves there. When churchgoers were unbearably cold, they went out during intervals of the service and warmed themselves in these Sabbath Day houses.

When stoves were later added to the old churches, some of the Sabbath Day houses still remained, but people sold refreshments and meals from them. Money was never allowed to pass hands on the Sabbath, so food was either paid for during the week or contributed free by the congregation. In either case, the convenience was appreciated because many churchgoers lived so far away that the weekly trip was a brave overnight pilgrimage which always induced hearty appetites. When there were no Sabbaday houses, local homes were usually thrown open for the purpose, and many a "house on the green" was known as a Sabbath Day house a century ago.

Great-grandfather's church has been condemned as embodying too much "hell fire and brimstone," but those who criticize forget that everything was done with more zest in the olden days. When Sunday came and the meeting house became a church, the preacher forgot all business and politics of the week and became an ardent revivalist. There were few quiet preachers. As a matter of fact, if you want to imitate an actor, preacher, salesman, or other character who might have lived a century ago, you can get the proper effect by

33

Four fireplaces

"*Sabbaday House* New Jersey, 1820

simply putting your everything into your act. In modern parlance this is known as "overdoing it."

The earliest colonial church services were solemn and quiet, much like a court of law. Both, incidentally, were announced by a roll of drums. But when church bells arrived and organs were installed, nineteenth-century sensationalism found expression even in the church. Revival meetings were particularly noisy, and when the national anthem was sung, drums and bells and even guns usually accompanied the singing.

In 1872 a religious festival advertised a chorus of twenty thousand voices and an orchestra of two thousand. Musical concerts could not survive without tableaux and spectacular sound effects. One concert had a hundred real anvils for a hundred men to pound on during the anvil chorus. Circuses by this time carried actual cannon with their bands. Here, for example, is the wording from a P. T. Barnum poster:

"National anthems by several hundred trained voices, accompanied by music and roar of cannon. I carry my own park of cannon and a large church bell. This circus fires a national salute of thirteen guns each morning accompanied by public bells, while the national anthem at night is sung to a cannonade of my whole park of cannon, a display of patriotic fireworks of Washington, American flags, etc., in red, white and blue."

One accomplishment of modern life is the art of not overdoing things. Another is doing several things at the same time. Many of us cannot enjoy breakfast nowadays without cereal-box labels to decipher while we eat. Some fathers seem to get the most out of the newspaper over the breakfast table and some mothers do their housework best with a soap-opera TV background. All this double action might be regarded as an amusing accomplishment if great-grandfather could come back and observe it. But still he would frown at such goings-on as letting a TV play or a speech by our President serve as the background for parlor conversation. Such present-day "accomplishments" are really bad habits. The child who can't sleep unless some program—any program!—is coming over the air will too often in later life be the slave of habit who removes his hat when a lady enters the elevator and puts it back on again when the elevator stops.

Theodore Roosevelt said the greatest thing he learned in school was to "do one thing at a time, and to concentrate on it." When great-grandfather removed his hat for a lady, he really put his heart into it, and the lady loved it. When the old-time minister preached, he really "went to town," and great-grandfather heartily approved.

From the day great-grandfather learned his alphabet, the discipline of the Bible became a part of his everyday life. Even the first alphabetical toy blocks were painted with Biblical illustrations. Wherever a reference to the Bible could be used, it seemed a natural accompaniment, no matter what the subject matter.

If there is any difference between the American churchgoer of today and his brother of a century or two ago, it might involve their reasons for going. Now that churches tend to decorate city life instead of being its hub, church learning has become more of an embellishment to living than its source.

The first churches were considered to be the main support in the structure of American life. An old New England name for the summer beam—the strongest beam of a house—was the "church beam"; it was this now-waning importance that the colonists gave the church. Today, if you ask an average person why he goes to church, he will invariably say, "To gain something." But when you ask him exactly what he expects to gain, he gropes for an answer. Great-grandfather did not go to church expecting to gain anything more than he already had; he went there to give thanks for it. In these competitive times, where the love of gain has penetrated everywhere, we are led to believe that we are going backward as soon as we cease to gain. It seems incredible to do anything, even to attend church, without profiting materially **35** from it. Great-grandfather had mastered the magnificent art of standing still.

Today we have all but forgotten the many religious sects which once

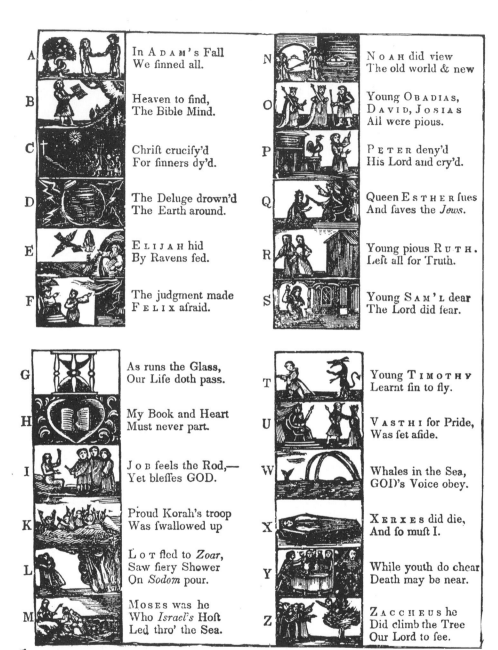

A	In ADAM's Fall We sinned all.	N	NOAH did view The old world & new
B	Heaven to find, The Bible Mind.	O	Young OBADIAS, DAVID, JOSIAS All were pious.
C	Christ crucify'd For sinners dy'd.	P	PETER deny'd His Lord and cry'd.
D	The Deluge drown'd The Earth around.	Q	Queen ESTHER sues And saves the *Jews*.
E	ELIJAH hid By Ravens fed.	R	Young pious RUTH. Left all for Truth.
F	The judgment made FELIX afraid.	S	Young SAM'L dear The Lord did fear.
G	As runs the Glass, Our Life doth pass.	T	Young TIMOTHY Learnt sin to fly.
H	My Book and Heart Must never part.	U	VASTHI for Pride, Was set aside.
I	JOB feels the Rod,— Yet blesses GOD.	W	Whales in the Sea, GOD's Voice obey.
K	Proud Korah's troop Was swallowed up	X	XERXES did die, And so must I.
L	LOT fled to *Zoar*, Saw fiery Shower On *Sodom* pour.	Y	While youth do chear Death may be near.
M	MOSES was he Who *Israel's* Host Led thro' the Sea.	Z	ZACCHEUS he Did climb the Tree Our Lord to see.

It began with your A, B, C's in those days

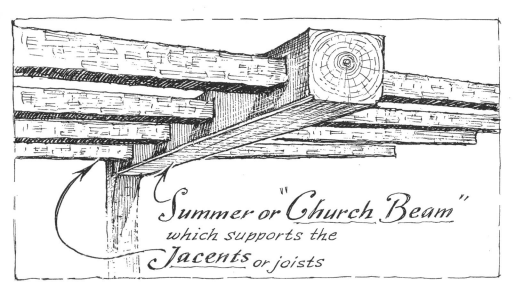

Summer or "Church Beam" which supports the Jacents or joists

sought to found their own little independent "nations" within America. Driven from Europe because of persecution and inspired by the success of the Pilgrims, these people built almost countless little "paradises" in almost every state. Pennsylvania possibly has the greatest scattering of such lost Utopias, although its Mennonites and Amish are the only commonly known "plain people" left.

Picking one of the old American Utopias at random, we might choose Harmony, Pennsylvania, where the Rappites built a complete town in ten years and sold it at a great loss. Or we might follow the Rappites to New Harmony, Indiana, where they built another town in ten years and sold it at another loss. Their next Utopian town was ironically named Economy, in Pennsylvania, but the end of the Rappites was by then already in sight when George Rapp, who had inspired the movement and believed in a second coming of Christ within his generation, died. Because the Rappites were bound to strict celibacy, with their men and women sleeping in separate dormitories, there were no children to replace the Rappites who died. But the empires of trade to which they gave birth and the towns they built will live on despite their pathetic contribution to the religions of vanished America.

Today, the white spires of yesterday's churches are among the few remaining symbols of America's past. The church and the farm were once pieces of each day's activity, but now they are becoming refuges. Whether it is the suburbanite whose big church day is Sunday or the city person who stops by during lunch hour to pray, there is always an element of escape from the business world. Perhaps great-grandfather overdid his religion with long graces at the table and group Bible readings before bedtime, but he derived more of God as a way of life than he could by regarding Him only as a refuge.

The Rappites who didn't believe in marked graves, were buried in walled enclosures

Great-grandfather's Home.

IT TAKES A THOUSAND men to get a load of fuel oil from the raw material to your furnace and probably as many to deliver a load of coal. It takes only one man, however, to make a pile of cordwood. Unlike a mess of oil or a heap of coal, a stack of wood is a living and a gladdening thing to behold. It has long been the symbol of the double benefits of farm life, warming you twice —once when you cut it, another when you burn it. Actually there is a third warming which is hard to define; an old almanac says, "City homes are warmed by coal, but country hearths do warm the soul."

The happy fact that the early American home and farm were one is much more than a casual commentary on colonial life. It was the pioneer's creed and a basic American belief until only a century ago. Today it has all but vanished. Like every American, Jefferson truly believed that "those who labor in the earth are the chosen people of God" and that "the farmer is the most noble and independent man in society."

Whether you were a banker or shoemaker in colonial times, you were always at the same time a farmer: whether your home was large or small, it was also a farmstead. Even princes and politicians and poets of the eighteenth century were ardent agriculturists or posed as farmers and rural philosophers. Not having a rural background and a farming philosophy in those times was perhaps as bad as not being a church member.

To a great extent, the size and condition of your land and barns influenced your standing in the community. This in many cases resulted in barns

The fuel that heats you twice.

being much bigger than necessary, particularly among the Dutch and the Germans who were least conservative architecturally and most competitive in spirit. Some of the Dutch and German barns were bigger than the great tithe-barns of ancient Europe, a fact which gave their owners great pleasure as New World farmers.

We think of George Washington as being a "gentleman farmer," which now describes a hobbyist, but Mount Vernon followed the tradition of all homes of that time. The General had the exact knowledge of farming that every American enjoyed as part of his daily life. How strange and foreign to modern living is a notation from the diary of John Adams: "Rose at sunrise, unpitched a load of hay and translated two more 'Leaves of Justinian.'"

Farming now is an occupational pursuit. Farmers raise stock to sell, but two centuries ago they farmed almost entirely for themselves. Instead of a pursuit, farming was then a way of life. The philosophy of farming, which was once a recognized American principle, was based upon three beliefs:

1. That agriculture is the fundamental employment of man upon which all other economic activities are vitally dependent.

2. That the farmer enjoys economic independence.

3. That farm life is the natural life and, being natural, is therefore good. (This belief implies that the completely city life is necessarily a corrupt one.)

The inference that city life is inescapably corrupt seems so foolish as to be childish. Yet only now are psychologists wondering how to return to the American morality of a century ago. Without our realizing it, the laws and regulations of city and industrial living have stripped us of the habit of taking

Dutch Barns were big . . . .

Schenectady
New York
1715

German Barns were bigger!

Pennsylvania
1760

responsibility for our own moral judgments. Guiding ourselves by polls and unions and what other Americans think, we base our decisions entirely upon what the majority does. A century ago when everyone took pride in being individual and different from the rest, the fact that many people cheat on income tax, practice race segregation, or use politics for their own personal gain would have been the last argument to justify our doing likewise. That would be just the time, in fact, for great-grandfather to polish his personal honor.

It is perfectly true that today's automobilist believes himself free to drive fifty miles an hour in a forty-mile zone, provided everyone else is doing the same, while the typical country driver is more careful about adhering to the law. It is true that the farmer would blush at the practice of putting down on his income tax report the "entertainment" and similar "expenses" which the city man enters. So, as childish as the remark might seem, your psychologist will prove that the city conformist is morally far behind the rural individualist.

Many features of the American home, from framing to shingles, were first used in barns. Barns, however, were designed to shrink and allow for ventilation during dry hot weather, but as homes improved, they became tighter and less drafty. The clapboard was the first refinement over barn design to grace the farmstead home. Clapboards, which are the simplest of outside house coverings today, were at first considered "dressy." Their earliest use was on the fronts of houses, while sides and backs were covered with

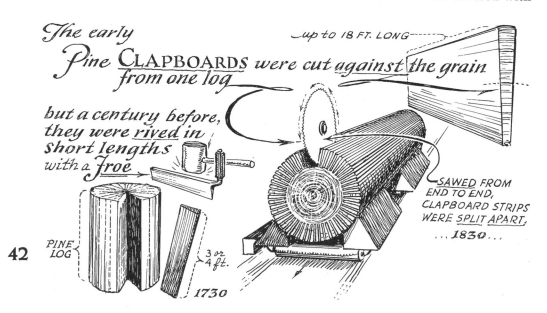

The early Pine CLAPBOARDS were cut against the grain from one log —up to 18 FT. LONG

but a century before, they were rived in short lengths with a froe

PINE LOG
3 or 4 ft.
1730

SAWED FROM END TO END, CLAPBOARD STRIPS WERE SPLIT APART. ...1830...

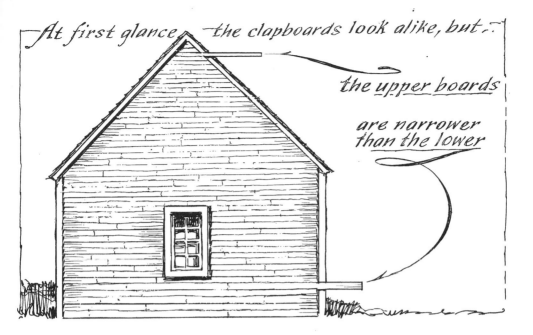

At first glance, the clapboards look alike, but... the *upper boards* are narrower than the lower

rough shingles. There is confusion about the origin of the word "clapboard" as the New England version was at one time called "clayboard," and some antiquarians insist clapboards once covered clay walls. But as the early Germans called them "Klappen Holz," the derivation seems more likely to have come from that source. ("Klappen" means to place or fit, while "Holz" is wood.)

The practice of clapboarding included such lost arts as cutting boards inward from one log (so there could be no warpage) and placing them upon the house in graduated widths. For example, many early gables were clapboarded according to dynamic symmetry, the widest boards at the bottom of the gable and lessening in width toward the peak. The difference is usually so slight as to be almost imperceptible, but that subtlety makes the difference all the more important and the builder that much more an artist. An effect of height is obtained by graduating clapboarding in this manner and many otherwise squat farmhouses have narrower boards toward the roof to give a pleasing effect. You might need a ruler to prove the difference, for perspective is deceptive. It is interesting and revealing to realize that the so-called simple farmer of yesterday knew these classic rules of symmetry, and that he considered them more important than does the average builder of today. Such variations have often been mistaken for the "imperfections of primitive carpentry." Consider the

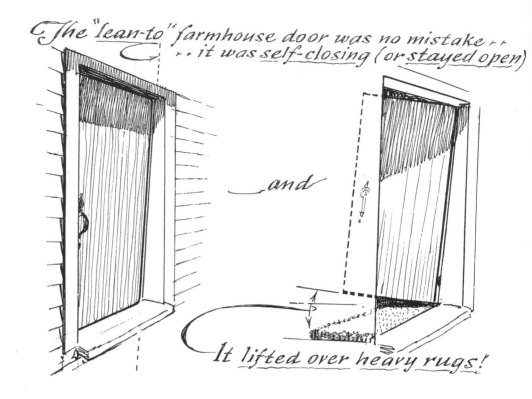

The "lean-to" farmhouse door was no mistake ·· ·· it was self-closing (or stayed open)

and

It lifted over heavy rugs!

plight of the New England lean-to door which is usually regarded as a mistake and replaced with a new door. It leaned so that almost no doorsill was necessary, and so it lifted itself over the heavy foot-wiping rug which was usually within the room. When you can't open a door because of an interfering rug, take the trouble to recall how great grandfather solved the problem.

At first the farmer had no more uniform of his profession (such as overalls, boots, and straw hat) than a business man would have now. It was the great divide of the Civil War and the machine age that shook the philosophy of farming and separated the farmer from the business man and the farm from the home. Those few who would have no part of change and continued in the old way became the "farmers" we knew only a few years back. They became the chin-whiskered, heavily booted Abners and Zekes who have so long been caricatured as "the American Farmer."

Farming is no longer a philosophy, but a full-time occupation. Whereas every American fed himself two centuries ago, only ten per cent of the population now feeds the other ninety per cent—and some portion of the rest of the world, too. Silas and all his things "down on the farm" are passing from the scene to join the vanished American landscape.

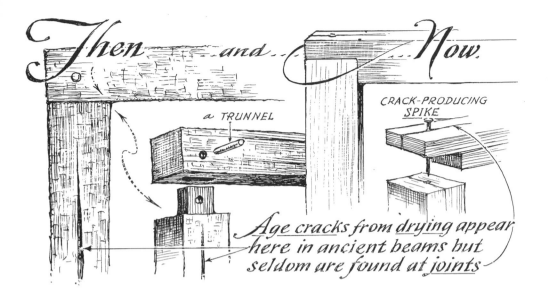

a TRUNNEL

CRACK-PRODUCING SPIKE

Age cracks from drying appear here in ancient beams but seldom are found at joints

If the covering were removed from old buildings, you would find the framework of the home and the barn exactly alike. The early method of fastening beams has never been improved upon; despite the contention that the "old fellows had all the time in the world," it is we with our time-savers who actually have more time. Using mortises and wooden pins is not just a slower way or a primitive way: it is the best way.

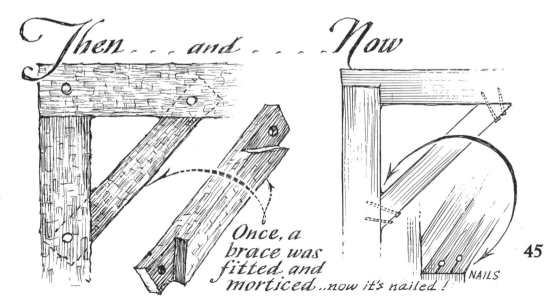

Then .... and .... Now

Once, a brace was fitted and morticed ..now it's nailed !

NAILS

45

History students are told that early settlers put timbers together with wooden pins because there were few nails to be had and those few were taxed by the Crown. The scarcity of metal and the taxes on hardware were real, but even if nails and spikes had been available, the wood-wise pioneer would have still used wooden pins. Much mention has been made of early houses being burned for their nails, but this occurred only during wartime. Often the nails remaining were not used as hardware at all, but melted down for bullets and implements. In all furniture and paneling, even when nails became plentiful, wood pins were still used, some as small as present-day brads. Most wooden nails or trunnels (tree-nails) were put in place hot and dry so that they might swell up with normal moisture and "weld" the joint together as they aged. As the drawing shows, nails tend to crack wood, while trunnels never cause cracks.

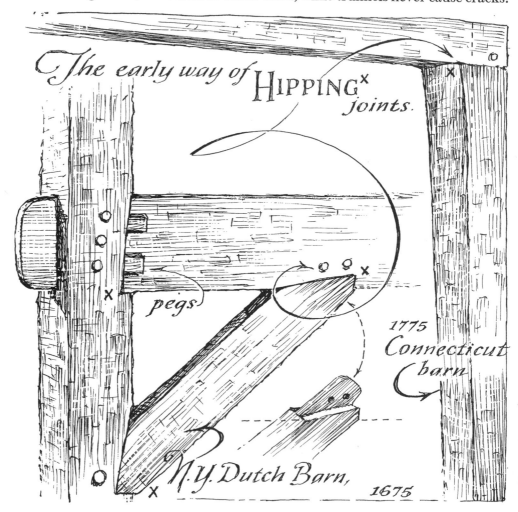

The early way of HIPPING[x] joints.

pegs

1775 Connecticut barn

N.Y. Dutch Barn, 1675

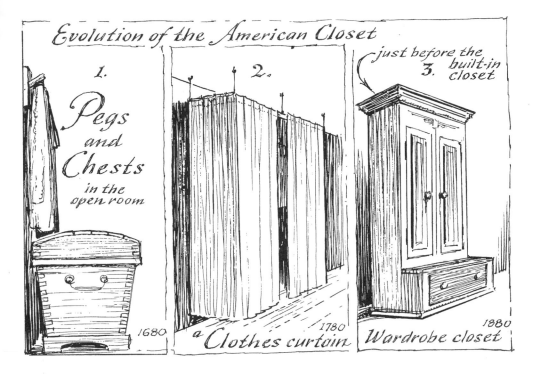

Evolution of the American Closet

1. *Pegs and Chests* in the open room

1680

2. a *Clothes curtain*

1780

just before the built-in closet 3.

Wardrobe closet

1880

Ancient timbers split with the dryness of age, but their joints and fastening-pins are usually left hard and crackless.

The ancient art of "shouldering" or "hipping" joints for extra strength was evident in the earliest pegged framework. The drawing shows hips at places marked X. The hip was often so slight as to be mistaken for an error in beam width: only the fact that all the rest of the beams were so treated reveals the truth.

Not long ago, few people were without an old homestead in their childhood background. But now when many people seem to change their home as often as they change their automobile, homes have become apartments or apartment-sized. Big homesteads have disappeared into rarity. Before the next century has passed, the typical American homestead will have become past history.

The average home of a century ago had twice as many extra rooms (most of which are now obsolete and forgotten) as are in the complete house of today. The smoke room, food cellar, borning room, milk room, chapel room, keeping room, summer kitchen, wash room, and corn room are just a few rooms that were as standard to an old house as a coat closet is to a modern one. Such a maze of rooms must have been fascinating to children; there is little wonder the old houses have lingered through growing-up memories and haunted us during later years.

By the 1900's most of the old homesteads' rooms had been eliminated. Some had become bedrooms for that "new institution," the servant girl. Others became closets, which were unknown before 1800.

The clothes closet as we know it today is an American invention. The "closet" was originally a private or secret room. Clothes were either hung in the open on pegs or folded into chests, each person having a personal chest, often at the foot of the bed. The only early American household enclosures were cupboards, and even they did not appear until the middle 1700's. In about 1780, American farm wives invented the idea of placing curtains (hung from a wire) to cover the clothing hanging on pegs. This arrangement waited only for the curtain to be replaced by wooden doors to give birth to the clothes

Plumbum-man 1700's or *Plumber* 1800's

Beating a Lead Pipe with a Lead-man's hammer

Pipe-mold   *Sheet Lead*

closet. If you have ever seen small iron hooks hanging from ancient bedroom ceilings and wondered what they were, they were probably there to hold "clothes curtains" during the pre-closet days.

Privies entered the house about 1800 by way of abandoned clothes closets and were appropriately called "water closets." When tubs were installed, however, a whole room became necessary and the American bathroom was born. Tubs were all different at first; they were designed entirely by carpenters and installed before adding lead covering and lead-pipe outlets.

In early days, when you wanted to buy lead, you used the Latin word and asked for so many pounds of "plumbum." The man who worked with lead, making rain gutters, surveyor's weights (plumb bobs), and kitchen sinks was called a "plumbum-worker." When sanitary engineering appeared just before the 1900's, everything metallic connected with it was made of lead. All metal pipes were made of lead; sinks and bathtubs were wooden boxes lined with sheet lead. Pipes were not threaded and screwed together, but joined with an overlapping layer of lead and "wiped" together. Wooden pipes were still being manufactured in 1875, but the lead worker or plumbum-man of the nineteenth century ended that industry and became the plumber of today, by way of the bathroom.

It is startling to realize that the bathtub, as we know it, is very recent. Many persons now living were once children in a world of no bathtubs other than small portable ones. One of the things that impresses visitors at the Sagamore, Long Island home of Theodore Roosevelt is its lonely tub. The President of the United States had to share one tub with his large family and the great number of notables who visited the estate. The fact, of course, was not that the President was stingy, but that tubs were rare then. Made to order and quite a new thing in the early 1900's, the President's wooden-boxed model was probably the envy of all who wallowed in its watery confines.

The first built-in bathtub is supposed to be that of Adam Thompson at Cincinnati, Ohio. It was seven feet long and four feet wide, cased in mahogany and lined with sheet lead, weighing close to a ton. It was filled with water through a hand pump. On December 20th, 1842, Thompson had a tub-christening party and all the guests were invited to try out the new "indoor bathpool." The newspaper stories that followed were characterized by attacks by doctors who said the practice of bathing in winter would cause chronic colds. However, the idea took hold among the wealthy. In many towns where the water supply was small, a thirty-dollar tax was levied on each bathtub, designed, of course, to discourage their use.

49

The change from lead worker to plumber came almost overnight. Although mass production built-in bathtubs did not appear until a couple of

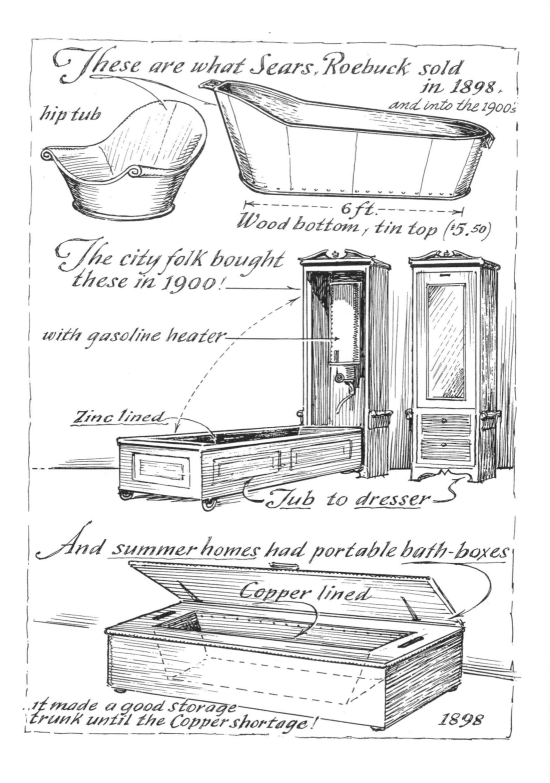

These are what Sears, Roebuck sold in 1898, and into the 1900's

hip tub

6 ft.

Wood bottom, tin top ($5.50)

The city folk bought these in 1900!

with gasoline heater

Zinc lined

Tub to dresser

And summer homes had portable bath-boxes

Copper lined

..it made a good storage trunk until the Copper shortage!

1898

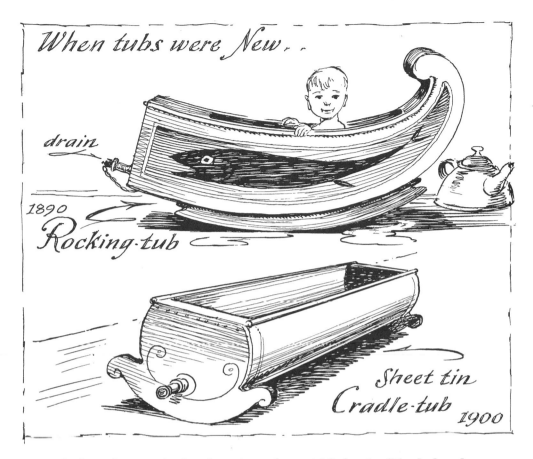

When tubs were New..

drain

1890
Rocking-tub

Sheet tin
Cradle-tub 1900

years before the 1900's, by that time the word "plumber" had already come to mean the same as "sanitary engineer." Lead is still used by plumbers for soldering connections, and their ladles and equipment are unchanged from those of two centuries ago. Today few plumbers know the origin of their title.

It seems that Saturday evening has always been bath night, but few of us know that it stems from a religious beginning. When the Sabbath started at sundown on Saturday, many people followed the adage that cleanliness and Godliness go together and bathed only at that time. Before bathrooms existed, cedar tubs were placed before the fireplace on Saturday, half-filled with cold water, while the kettle of hot water to be added later hung over the fire. Some of the first portable tin tubs even had Biblical quotations painted upon them, but not many people would now associate a bathtub with the Sabbath. **51**

The first tubs, like any other new-fangled gadget, assumed strange shapes. Some were made with "hips" to fit the shape of the body. Some were painted with scenic designs, some were decorated solidly with floral patterns. Among the oldest was the cradle-tub for children to splash and rock in while taking their bath.

The cradle, which is one of the earliest standard pieces of furniture, has now passed into obsolescence in America. If you went out to purchase a cradle you would be disappointed, for they are no longer made. The last cradle manufactured was made over fifty years ago. The reason for the disappearance of cradles from the household scene is an American mystery, for they are still made in Europe and children need and enjoy the pleasant motion of rocking. Books on child care suggest rocking, but they do not say how they should be rocked, unless they imply that the child is to be held in a rocking chair!

At one time or another, cradles have been attached to butter churns, turnspits, dog mills, and even windmill gears to give them automatic movement, but the simple rocker cradle remained in the American household for over two centuries before its disappearance. People now prize antique cradles for storing magazines; it seldom occurs to them to put them to their proper use.

One of the more disputed examples of early American rocking furniture is the "adult cradle." It is sometimes argued that a few examples which are over six feet long were intended as cradles for twins, arranged so that the babies could lie end-to-end instead of side-by-side. Some have been used by new mothers and babies at the same time, while others have been occupied by senile or invalid persons. At any rate, they are known as "adult cradles"; they are just about the size of a single bed, but built closer to the floor.

The rocking chair is a purely American idea. We have had them since 1774, whereas the earliest known foreign rocker was made in 1840. The word "rocker" did not mean a chair until recently, but it did refer to those curved pieces of wood beneath cradles. Originally rocking chairs were called rocker chairs.

The step from cradle to rocking chair is lost in the complexity of American inventiveness that flourished between 1750 and 1775. There was once a combination cradle and settee known as a "rockee" or "rocking settee" that might have been the missing link between the two pieces of furniture.

Almost all of the early straight-backed rocking chairs are converted chairs with rockers added. Benjamin Franklin had experimented with an iron rocker to fasten to any chair. He also had a most remarkable "chair with rockers, and a large fan placed over it with which he fanned himself, keeping flies off, etc., while he sat reading, with only a small motion of his foot."

52   One of great-grandfather's achievements was his discovery of comfort. Colonial comfort, like its medieval interpretation, was mostly in a "satisfaction of space and proportions." Chairs were all hard and flat, while beds were

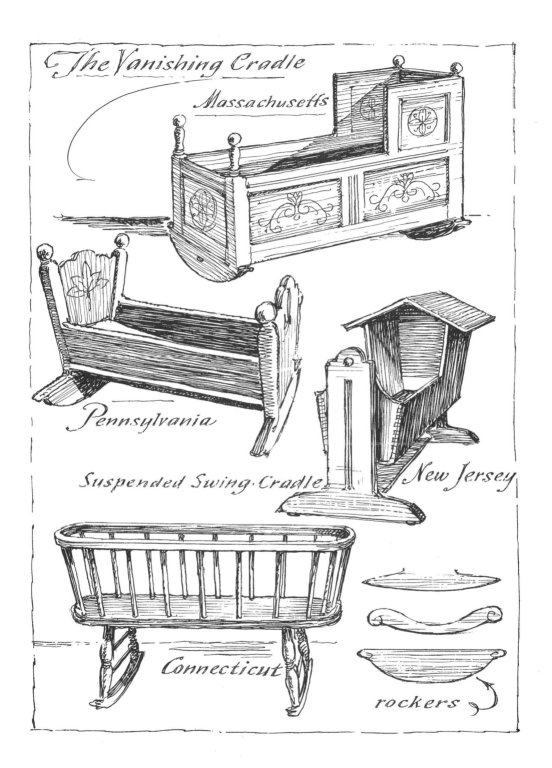

The Vanishing Cradle

Massachusetts

Pennsylvania

Suspended Swing Cradle

New Jersey

Connecticut

rockers

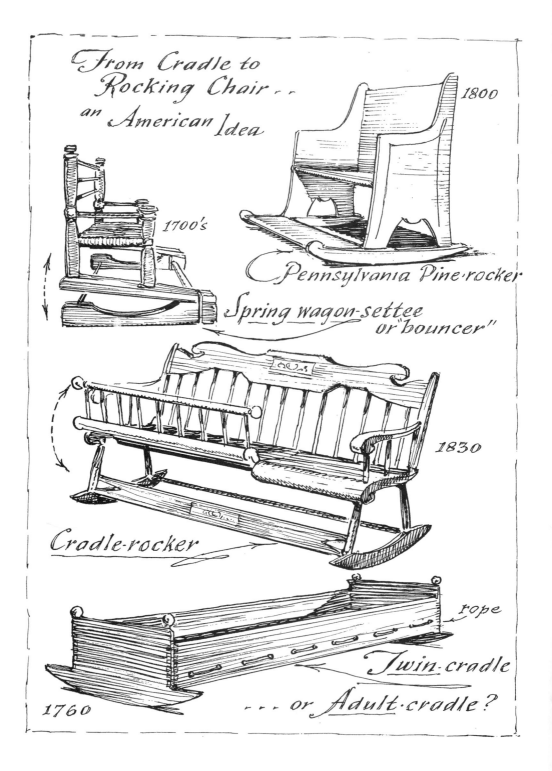

From Cradle to Rocking Chair...
an American Idea

1800

1700's

Pennsylvania Pine-rocker

Spring wagon-settee or "bouncer"

1830

Cradle-rocker

rope

Twin-cradle

1760

...or Adult-cradle?

not much better. The American rope bed was considered the ultimate in comfort.

The rope-strung torture machine in which our ancestors slept suited the times very well, and it likewise seemed to suit its occupants. When you realize that most of the early beds were entirely home-made, their slight efficiency and comfort seem all the more remarkable. The early days were so much more active than the present ones that sleep fortunately must have been quicker and sounder.

Many antique shops sell wooden "butter paddles" with handles that slant to one side instead of extending straight outward. This is often confusing until one realizes that they are not butter paddles at all, but bed-patters. Feather

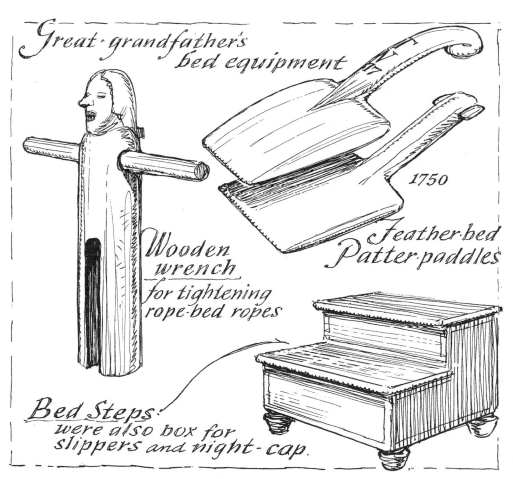

Great-grandfather's bed equipment

Wooden wrench for tightening rope-bed ropes

1750

Feather-bed Patter-paddles

Bed Steps: were also box for slippers and night-cap.

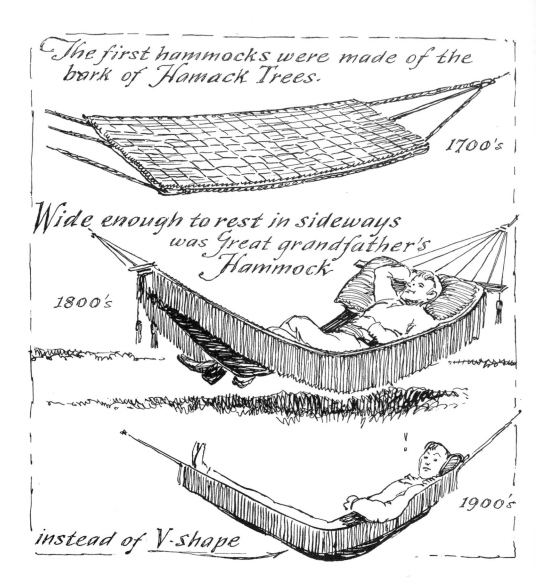

The first hammocks were made of the bark of Hamack Trees.

1700's

Wide enough to rest in sideways was Great grandfather's Hammock

1800's

1900's

instead of V-shape

beds needed a good deal of banging and patting to get them back into shape after a night's sleep on them, and a flat paddle to do the job was part of bedroom equipment. If you find a large paddle in your collection of wooden kitchenware, and wonder why it is dated or initialed, it is probably an eighteenth-century wedding gift, for bed-patters were once a favored present for the new bride.

The oldest rooms looked finished even when they were unfurnished: their comfort was visual rather than physical. The early twentieth century added

56

lounging porches to farmhouses, with rocking chairs and cushioned furniture to match. It became an age of featherbeds and padding. Indoor and outdoor comfort was the nineteenth-century order of the day.

One of the delights of those times was the hammock, which was a fringed joy compared to the skimpy examples available today. Perhaps it is a scarcity of trees for support that makes the old-fashioned hammock nearly obsolete, but the fact that the hammock is possibly the only type of furniture entirely native to the American continent should make it worthy of preservation. In 1492, when Columbus reached the western shores, one of the things which impressed him about the natives was their hammocks, in which a whole family often slept. When we rest in our present model, we recline lengthwise and assume an uncomfortable V shape, but the earliest hammocks were much wider and made for resting partly crosswise and nearly horizontal.

The early American house design is immediately recognizable by its outline or silhouette alone, and the reason is interesting. Houses used to be shapes divided into rooms, whereas houses have since become rooms massed into shapes.

The result of this early method of house-planning was a completely serviceable design. It gave immediate thought to roof slant, dynamic proportions, and pleasing over-all form. The modern method of planning often results in a ramble of disconnected shapes, in a one-story model or a two-story box-like shape with an unrelated roof. Today, when we design a home, we first decide the number and sizes and arrangements of rooms, then fit them into "a proper shape." Yesterday, Dutch gambrelled-squares, Duxbury-barn types, Cape Cod fisherman boxes, Pennsylvania penthouses, Virginia five-part mansions, New Hampshire joined houses, adobe ranch houses, New England garrison houses, and Southern plantation houses were all *basic shapes* to be divided into rooms. The major contribution to standard home design today is possibly "ranch house modern," which is less a style than it is an identification for a one-floor grouping of rooms.

So-called modern design is too often less inspired by the times than it is an escape from things traditional. Pure beauty is seldom the result of escape. With nothing to escape from, the good old homes were inspired by satisfaction of life and heritage, and revealed this quality. The finished product was lasting and good to look at, outliving architectural vogues.

Designers who have used the word "functional" as an explanation for their modernistic efforts have often been embarrassed to find their work identical to early American things which were functional without being at all obvious or calling for explanation. It is like a man traveling far in search of what he needs and returning home to find it there.

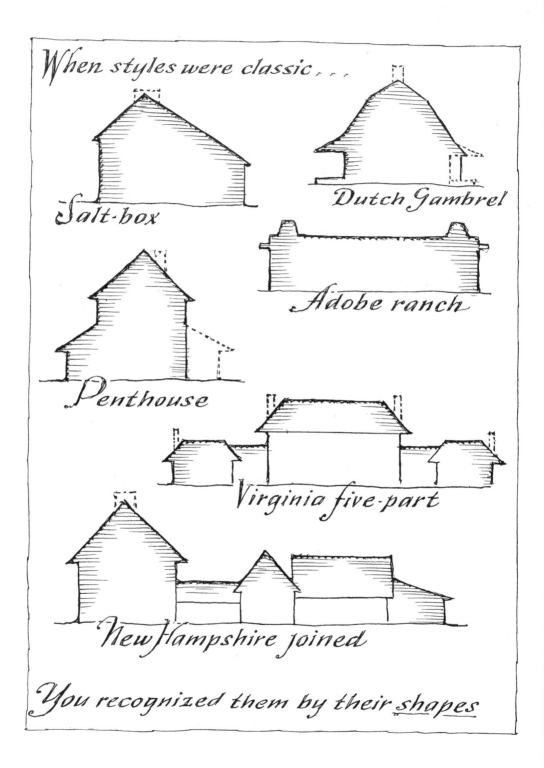

When styles were classic . . .

Salt-box

Dutch Gambrel

Penthouse

Adobe ranch

Virginia five-part

New Hampshire joined

You recognized them by their shapes

The nineteenth-century architects who produced what we call "Victorian" were important factors in America's first industrial era. The machine age seemed to call for a change in architecture; true to the American fallacy that any escape from the past or anything new must necessarily be progressive, the change was made. What resulted was a battle of styles that produced somewhat theatrical interpretations of Tudor, Gothic, Italian villa, Swiss chalet, Egyptian, and so on, into an endless list of the historical garbs of architecture. It even invaded the engine room and the plumbing.

There seems to be one outstanding characteristic of American Victorian, however (and one which has not been satisfactorily explained), called "gingerbread." We call it that because there is no definite word for the fretwork of scrolled wood that adorns most examples of this style of architecture. It has been called "Steamboat Gothic," "Belvidere," "Ice Cream," "Bargeboard Scroll," "Carpenter's Gothic," and other terms which denote ornateness in wooden trim. Its true name still remains as hidden as the identity of the forgotten carpenters who created it. Very often gingerbread scroll was not included in the building plans any more than rubber plants or bric-a-brac would be included in interior plans, but was added during construction. In some cases, it was even added years later to "modernize" farmhouses. The fact that gingerbread scroll appeared at the same time as the carpenter's ribbon saw (later to be known as the bandsaw) explains much.

The early northern farmhouse bedrooms and our present-day bathroom had much in common in both size and shape. A farmhouse room in those days

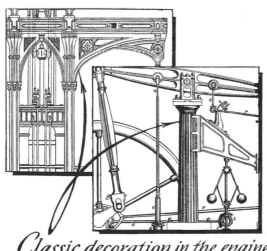

Classic decoration in the engine-room

59

was just what the word "room" denotes—space for a purpose: every room was self-contained and maintained its own integrity. Halls which allowed a cell-like division of small rooms have since been eliminated wherever possible; the old "bedroom hallway" is joining the list of vanishing rooms. This list has just about reached its maximum now that homes have achieved a uniform minimum of size. Here are some of those rooms which were all-important yesterday, but which will never find their way back into an architect's plan:

Wash Room:

Laundry. In the South, this was situated outside the house and under a shed. In New England, it was a room or shed off the kitchen, often within the breezeway between the kitchen and the woodshed.

Smoke Room:

Always next to the main chimney, often on the second floor between bedrooms, more often in the attic. Here hams and meats were smoked over smoldering hickory shavings and ashes. Even farms which possessed outdoor smokehouses often had an attic smoke room.

Keeping Room:

A "heart-of-the-house room" where, during great storms, all living could be confined. Often the kitchen, but sometimes a general sitting room.

Before central heating, cellars were for food, and often not beneath the house

house

Protruding Shelf Supports

Cool in summer, far enough below the Ground not to freeze in Winter.

an Attic Smoke-room

L.I.,N.Y.
1780

main Chimney

Pillion Room:

On the first floor, near the kitchen. Used for women's saddles, whips, harnesses, blankets, and riding accessories not associated with farm horses and farming equipment.

Powdering Room:

The smallest room. Not the "powder room" of today, but used for the keeping and powdering of wigs. Once equipped with wig stands.

Loom Room:

Where weaving, spinning, and reeling were done. Usually a separate house in the South, often found in the back or under the great northern slant of New England saltbox houses.

Cellar:

In its true use, cellar is a word from the French meaning food storage **61** room. It was located beneath the house only to keep food cool during summer and to protect it against freezing in the winter. The first cellars were not under the house at all, but a few steps away from it. They were underground rooms, sometimes with an opening into the well pit so that cool, damp air could enter. You will find evidence that ancient cellars served as storage pantries by the discovery of protruding stones in the cellar walls designed to support massive shelves.

Cock Loft:

A room above the garret. Garrets were used for so many things that a ceiling was often put in, making them separate rooms in their own right, with a small garret overhead.

Open Chamber:

Sometimes referred to as the season room. The large unfinished upper story of a house which was left to whatever use might arise, according to the time of year. In winter it stored corn and hides. In summer it was the hired hand's room, the "boy's room," or the chest room for clothing. Often referred to in Vermont diaries as the "corne loft."

Chapel Room:

A small room-closet, usually at the front of the house, used for meditating. A surprising number of plain farmhouses had chapel rooms which have since become forgotten and converted into closets.

Invalid Room:

A room hidden away in the back of the house with entrance only through the kitchen; intended for invalids, but most often for the member of the

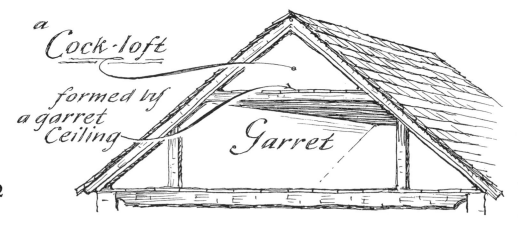

family "not quite right." It was considered better to keep weak-minded relatives at home with the family instead of committing them to institutions, particularly when they were aged. In many old farmhouses these rooms were known only by the invalid's name, such as "Aunt Jenny's room" or "Old Pete's room," etc.

Captain's Room:

A small room on top of a flat-topped monitor roof. Originally used by sea captains or their wives for watching ships arrive in the harbor. When railed around, it was called a "captain's walk" or "widow's walk."

Buttery:

A room for provisions off the kitchen, often a milk room or place for the making and storing of cheeses. Here the churn and cheese cloths were kept. Milk rooms were missing in the earliest houses, and so was milk. Cows were kept mainly to breed oxen; cider and beer were drunk at the dinner table, even by children, who seldom tasted cow's milk.

Dumbwaiter (or Butler's) Pantry:

A turn-of-the-century room off the dining room for the "dumbwaiter" or rope elevator which transported food and dishes from the kitchen below to the upper floors of brownstone-type houses in the city.

Borning Room:

Usually off the kitchen, an ancient room reserved for births. Often used as a sick room and for placing tubs for Saturday bathing.

Hot-Water Pantry:

A closet near the kitchen where water was heated in a big iron pot. This pot was often located over the fire where the coals for baking ovens were prepared. The pantry (from the French word for bread) was also a room for keeping bread. The moist effect of heating water kept bread fresh and tasty, so the two rooms were combined and bread was stored in the hot-water pantry, along with dough and baking equipment.

Summer Kitchen:

A room separate from the house, but usually attached by a breezeway, where all cooking was done during the warmer months. The kitchen fireplaces and ovens operated twenty-four hours a day, causing considerable heat during the warm months. Breakfast, which was usually indistinguishable from supper, was often started at night so it might be cooked by morning.

Spring Room:

Often a part of the kitchen, sometimes a dropped room just off the

Hot-water Pantry

Stone shelves

Hot water pot

FLUE

Fire for preparing Oven Coals

kitchen. Here spring water constantly flowed into a giant barrel and overflowed into an outlet that carried it downhill and away.

64 As the farm grew and the family increased, many of the old rooms became outbuildings and they, too, were placed with some forethought and planning. When great-grandfather chose his home site, he built into a plot of air as well as upon a plot of ground. Weatherwise and aware of the effects of weather on buildings and farm stock and humans, he determined the position of his home and barn and outbuildings by the disposition of the land with regard to the prevailing winds and to the arc of the sun.

Wind dictates the mechanics of all fireplaces; therefore, it governed the comfort of early houses during winter. Long before the pick and ax fell, weather sites were researched and planned carefully. You will still find houses and barns molded into the weathered contours of the land, their roofs slanted steepest toward winter winds and their most lived-in rooms facing the warm south.

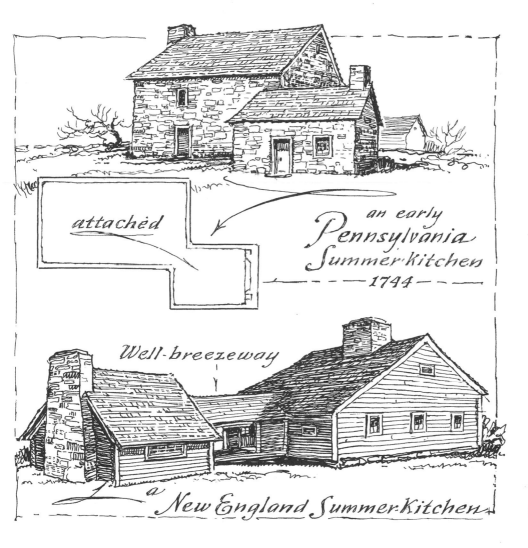

attached

an early *Pennsylvania Summer-Kitchen* — 1744 —

Well-breezeway

a *New England Summer-Kitchen*

65

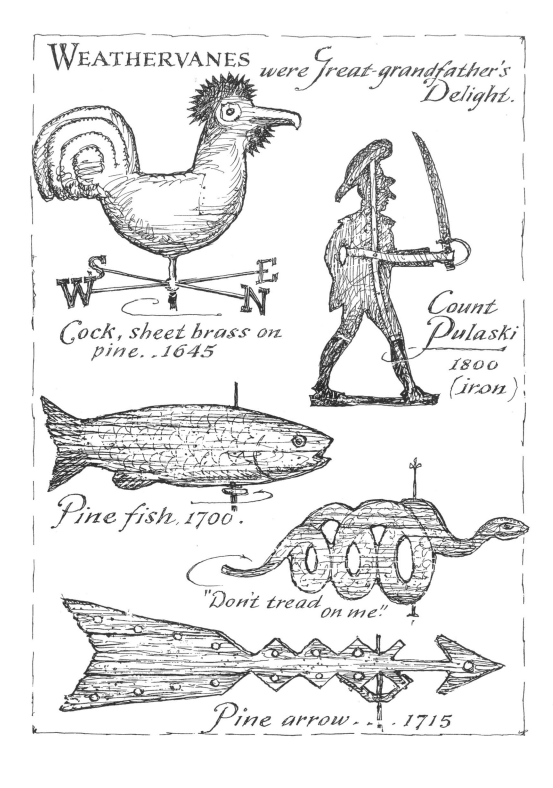

WEATHERVANES *were Great-grandfather's Delight.*

Cock, sheet brass on pine . . 1645

Count Pulaski 1800 (iron)

Pine fish, 1700.

"Don't tread on me!"

Pine arrow 1715

The weathervane which decorated all ancient barns was not a decoration as much as a farm implement. When to plant, when to cut hay, almost every act of farming in some way or other involved the direction of the wind. Barns, farm outbuildings, and privies were placed where prevailing summer winds could carry odors away, while honeysuckle and herb gardens were put where the same wind would carry sweet scents into the house.

The earliest weathervanes were made of dry, light pine, which explains why so few of them are still in existence. It was the custom for settlers first to use a strip of cloth as a wind pennant (vane is from the early word "fano" for flag), and to whittle a fine wooden weathervane during the first winter. The quadrants indicating north, east, south, and west were not used on early farm vanes because the barn itself was placed with its sides to the cardinal points and the farmer knew his wind directions instinctively.

When the 1800's brought in the vogue of painting houses, all sorts of decorations were added and iron weathervanes appeared by the thousands. Sheet copper was hammered over pine to make molded figures, but they were heavy and swung poorly in the wind. Later, however, after pounding the metal to a wooden shape, the inner wooden shape was removed; the result was a lighter hollow copper figure which swung easily. So the hollow weathervane, such as is still made today, was born.

The second most important thing about choosing a home site and arranging the early buildings was the water supply. Dug wells are comparatively recent, and the oldest houses had a constant gravity supply of spring water. Some farmhouses still have gravity spring water and they enjoy a supply even when the electric power fails or ordinary water systems become frozen. The contentment of hearing your own clear spring trickle into your house is fast becoming a vanished pleasure of the olden days.

A few antique shops still have examples of wooden pumps, but there is little interest in or market for them. Within another decade or two they will have become forgotten Americana. The pumpmaker was a very important man in the early village and he was always looked to for having special "water-finding" abilities. He was always an expert dowser.

"Dowsing," "divining," or "water-witching" was carried on as a regular occupation, although most farmers professed some ability to locate underground water. They held a forked willow stick in both hands and walked over the spring site; a sudden mysterious pull was supposed to be exerted upon the witching-stick, directing one to the nearest water. The first sticks were made of swamp hazel (hence the name witch hazel), but when willow (which English dowsers had always used) was imported to America, witching-sticks were then fashioned from this wood.

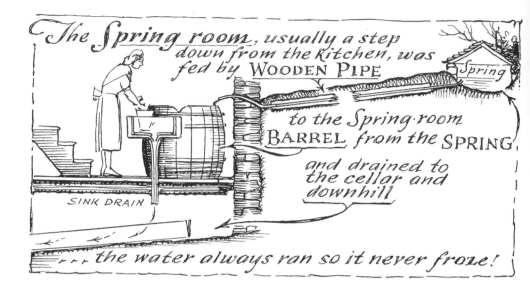

The Spring room, usually a step down from the Kitchen, was fed by WOODEN PIPE to the Spring-room BARREL from the SPRING and drained to the cellar and downhill

SINK DRAIN

Spring

...the water always ran so it never froze!

Well-building was not always a full-time job, particularly when the ground was frozen, so the pumpmaker spent his winter turning pump stocks and handles. He also specialized in dry-wall building. Dry-masoning began to disappear when cement entered on the American building scene. Hitherto, a good dry mason could build a permanent foundation wall without any bonding cement at all and could make it so tight and strong that two centuries have left the old foundations unmoved. Ask for a dry mason in any rural dis-

Well-diggers were expert with the Divining Rod

WELLS dug by GEO. OTT

Old sign from Roslyn L.I.

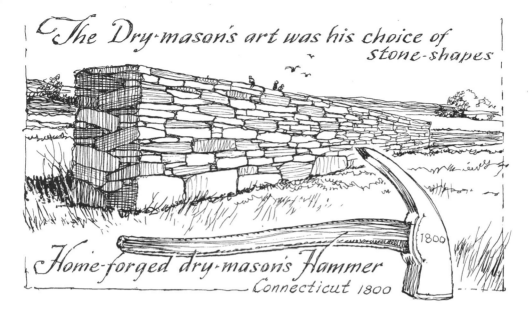

The Dry-mason's art was his choice of stone-shapes

Home-forged dry-mason's Hammer
— Connecticut 1800

trict in America and people will know what you are talking about. Furthermore, you will still find these men have the inherent knack of placing the right stone in the right place. Yet the art is a vanishing one and the name "dry mason" has already disappeared from dictionaries.

You might wonder why dry masonry and other obsolete occupations are not properly gone and forgotten. But we are not comparing building styles as much as we are discussing the builders themselves. It is revealing that the common worker of a few years ago did all his jobs "the hard way" and with an eye toward their lasting qualities, thinking almost less of his own lifetime than that of his successors. Our white population now averages two or three children in a family, but in the early nineteenth century women produced an average of eight, which might explain the passion for permanency.

Today one could hardly build anywhere and be certain that the area would not change within a few decades or that a highway might not come through sooner. There is no doubt that people used to build for their children's children, while the basic philosophy of present-day building (outside of immediate needs) is "What will I lose or gain if I sell?" It is interesting to learn from the termite-control companies how well some of the older places were built. "In houses of about two hundred years," they say, "the decay or eaten wood almost always has started in newer additions. Woodsheds or other structures added within the last fifty years are the source of our biggest business."

The first dry masons learned their art by making chimneys. Chimneys were made of mud and sticks when roofs were thatched, making both roofs and fireplaces dangerously flammable. With a little political pull, a dry mason could get the job of chimney-viewer and earn about eighty dollars a year (at present-day values) checking all the chimneys in town to prevent fire hazards. The first chimney-viewers were appointed by the Crown and they also became tax assistants wherever houses were taxed by the number of their chimneys. When colonists built houses and several fireplaces around one monstrous chimney, it was probably fireplaces and not chimneys which were taxed. But the work and title of chimney-viewer continued in many places until long after the Revolution.

Great-grandfather had his own special windows. We still use shutters "for decoration," although they once were opened every morning and closed

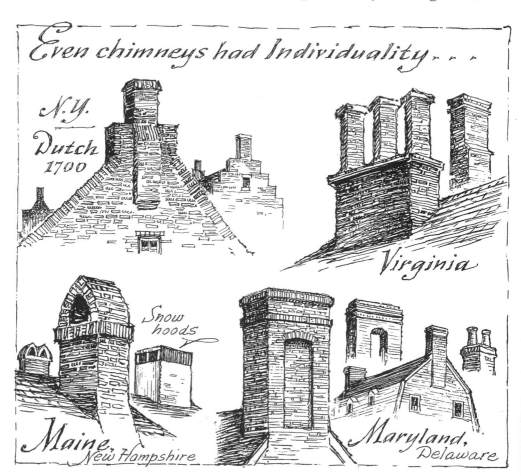

Even chimneys had Individuality . . .

N. Y. Dutch 1700

Virginia

Snow hoods

Maine, New Hampshire

Maryland, Delaware

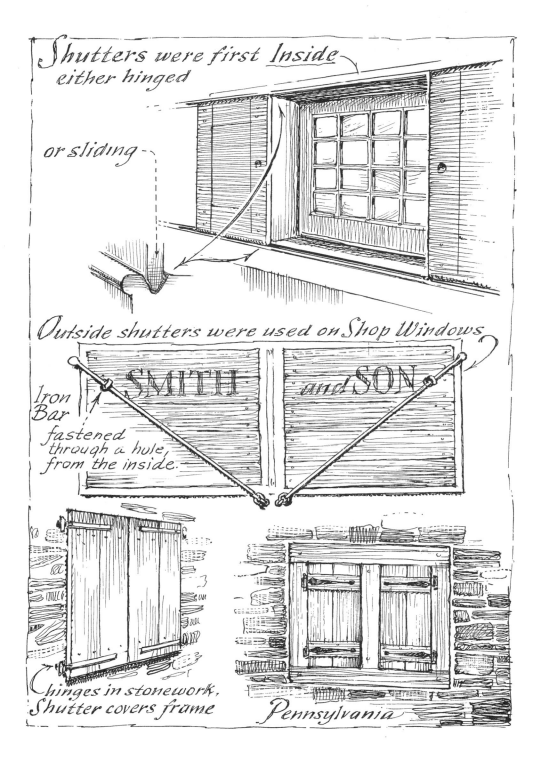

Shutters were first Inside
either hinged

or sliding -

Outside shutters were used on Shop Windows

SMITH and SON

Iron Bar fastened through a hole, from the inside.

hinges in stonework, Shutter covers frame

Pennsylvania

every night. Storekeepers "put up the shutters" as soon as night arrived; being too large for hinges, they were kept in back of the store during business hours. The scarcity of glass made early windows poor substitutes for what we have today, but, architecturally speaking, the beauty of old American windows will never be recaptured by the mass-production methods that seem necessary for modern building. We might think it strange or quaint to learn that the old-timers sold their houses or even rented them "less windows," carrying these around as special possessions. Yet the building wreckers' most prized merchandise now comprises old casement windows and attic "lights": modern builders buy them quickly, for they cannot be reproduced today with the same grace and workmanship.

a Window Sundial

The small New England windows with sashes that are never fastened but cling with nails half driven into the side casing were made thus so that windows could be removed or tightened easily. Most people hammer the nails in all the way with some annoyance at "the old way of doing things," but find trouble during winter when wood shrinks and the rattling windows need tightening. Others wonder at the cuts on window sills, often accompanied by numbers. These were indoor sundials for use in the days when a stopped clock could not be reset as easily as it is today; the shadow of a window strip on the sill could be depended on to tell fairly accurate time.

Great-grandfather's house would certainly not be sufficient for present-day living, but we might wonder if present-day living is sufficient itself. As time unwinds the clock, old houses are still sound emblems of gracious living. We may live more easily or casually nowadays, but there is a graciousness in hard work and chores that is beyond present-day comprehension. The building of a log fire and the task of watching and poking it is a pleasure which no steam radiator can replace. And the nervousness created by company moving from place to place in a room, glasses in hand, was missing from the early living room where everyone gravitated to the fireplace group.

Some ancient houses seem to speak like humans, even though they are empty. Yet most modern houses without furniture or people in them have no more character than a closet or a bathroom wall.

"The severe simplicity of the ultra-modern living room," says one designer, "is a suitable theatre for the dynamic character of today's personality." Such a statement causes one to pause and reflect.

Great-grandfather's Town.

A BLIND PERSON might say that living in the city is almost unbearable, while living in the country is a great adventure. Of course, in thinking of country living, we immediately recall its scenic values. Yet places, even one town from another, can also be identified by sound. Most of us are unaware of such slow change, but any age, even the decade we live in, may be identified by its sounds.

In the 1700's, the tread of heavy boots on wide plank floors, the ring of felling axes through the hills, the occasional roll of drums, the call of peddlers and town criers in the square, all identified the time. Each room had the sputter and hiss of fireplace logs; the kitchen had a tiny, comforting tinkle of water into a spring barrel. The whirr and clatter of spinning wheels and farm mills lasted throughout the day, but the wash of water through mill sluiceways and the faraway booming of back-country plumping mills lasted throughout the night.

In the 1800's there were church bells and door bells and bells on horses and cows and oxen. Lighter-weight button shoes were quieter as they walked on carpeted floors, but hoofbeats in the street clattered hollow and sharp on the new cobblestones. The sound of travel became one of wagon wheels over gravel roads and the booming roar of plank roads. Every bridge thundered its loose planks as the stagecoach passed over it. Kitchen stoves clattered their iron lids, the noise of plates was more brittle than the soft clash of pewter. All the noises of the early ovened fireplace were absent. The walking of people on stone sidewalks was the first "big city sound," second to the metallic

74

"Home, Sweet Home". . . Long Island, N.Y.

screech of street car rails or the whistles of trains and factories. "The noise of the city," an 1850 *Harper's Magazine* said, "is so strange to the farmer that it takes a few days of country quiet for him to get over the nervous tension."

The 1900's introduced new machine noises. The suburban clatter and clack of lawnmowers, the sputter and bang of the first automobiles, and the tinkle of pianos invaded the noises of rural home life. The city had by then developed its own noise—a hum which reached a nervous roar by day and settled to a more slumbering breathing hush by nightfall.

Spring-Barrel Symphony

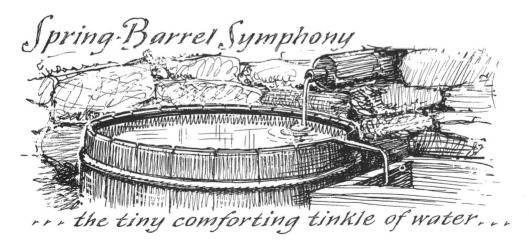

. . . the tiny comforting tinkle of water . . . 75

We are already accustomed to jet-plane noises. What would have troubled us twenty years ago has become no more than a sound backdrop for normal conversation today. We accept radio sounds without even analyzing them; only when they become so loud as to drown out conversation do we begin to notice them. Indeed, there is considerable sound-difference between the world of yesterday and the world of today.

It might be believed that great-grandfather enjoyed the sounds of his world more because he knew what they were. Today when we accept the pattern of city noise as an undercurrent or unnoticed sound of living (like that of our own breathing), we do so because to listen and identify each individual sound would be impossible. But the past joy of having to contend with only a few uninterrupted sounds made bird song, farm sounds, hearthside sounds, and each person's voice the appreciable music of everyday life. Yesterday there were sounds; today there is noise.

The noisiest part of yesterday's community was the town market. The best salesman was usually the loudest crier; if you had no "crying" ability, you could always hire it. Professional criers were the vaudevillians of their day, sometimes dressing in strange costumes, throwing in whatever talents they possessed, and often selling on a commission basis. You will hear about

Crying in the Market

The Head-House of Philadelphia's Second St. Market

old-time street vendors who "cried their wares," but these were usually professional criers who worked side by side with the actual salesman.

New York and other big cities still have a few crying vendors, such as the flower-wagon man who cries "flower plants," the rag merchant who cries "I cash clothes" (frequently just an abbreviated "I cash!"), and others selling ice, vegetables, etc. But all such "salesmen" were once frowned upon in any place but the town market and it was there that you could choose, from an always available group, the man to cry your wares.

Often in early records there will be mention of a "market master"; antiquarians have found little clue as to the meaning of this occupation. In 1952, while plans were under way to demolish Philadelphia's "Head House" in the Second Street Market, the office of market master was brought to light and as quickly eliminated from the city payroll. This long, narrow one-story structure had been in operation since it was built by the first mayor of Philadelphia, Edward Shipen, in 1745. It was one of the last of the old "middle-of-the-street markets."

Few people know that the very wide streets in the old business sections of some cities are wide because there was once a middle-of-the-street market there. Philadelphia and Boston and New York owe many of their wider streets to these outdoor markets which were managed by market masters. The city market master, like the country miller, was lawyer and banker to the farmer, who usually preferred trading merchandise instead of selling it. The market bell sounded the end of the business day but, because farmers usually drove all night to arrive near daylight, there was no opening signal for the day's trading. Every market had its bell, however, which closed the market day at sundown. Selling after hours was punished by a fine, imposed on both buyer and seller and payable to the market master.

Selling on the Sabbath likewise drew a strict fine and that was the only Holy Day or "Holiday" so observed by law. Holidays will never vanish from the American scene, but their meanings often become distorted with the years. Like the little boy who remarked how nice it was "that Christ happened to be born on Christmas Day," many of us are ignorant of the meaning of our holidays. The "Christmas rush," the "Easter parade," the "Thanksgiving feast," and all the other descriptive American holiday phrases convey meanings which are sometimes the opposite of their original significance. It is revealing to compare our present holidays with those of a century or two ago, before commercialism intervened.

Knowing that this country was founded on early religious principles, most people believe that Christmas is one of our first and greatest holidays. But the holy days of the English Church were completely ignored by the

Puritans and the one they hated most happened to be Christmas! When the Church of England established Christmas services in Boston, the majority rose against it, forbidding their children to attend. The Christmas celebration took a long while to evolve in America, and the Noël we know could not be regarded as a New England holiday until the nineteenth century.

The first New England Thanksgiving service was performed in the Church of England by the Popham colonists at Menhegan. Neither the Plymouth Pilgrim nor the Boston Puritan observed Thanksgiving at that time, although everyone seems to think they did. The final Puritan Thanksgiving lasted a week (not a day) devoted to feasting and gaming, without any record of special religious services.

Thanksgiving Day was never New England's big holiday. Writing in 1699, Ward does not even name it. "Election Day, Commencement Day and Training Day are their only Holy Days," he explains. "If the college die," the theory went, "the church cannot live." So Commencement Day was one of America's favorite holidays, although few of us are now aware of it. Much of our present holiday cooking originated with Commencement cake, Commencement puddings, and other Commencement Day delicacies.

Training Day, of course, was a military exercise, although it came closest to our present Fourth of July. When the Fourth came into being, many of the public shooting matches, "exercising of arms," and military din-

Independence Day was America's Picnic Day.

ners of the old Training Day were carried over into the new Independence Day celebration. The first Fourth of July in many ways resembled today's Thanksgiving Day, except that the feasting was in the form of outdoor picnicking.

In a New Milford, Connecticut barn there is an old newspaper, glued to cover the wall cracks, in which there is an account of a Fourth of July military luncheon. The toast mentioned therein gives insight into the average villager's conception of that holiday:

"July 6, 1822.

". . . at one o'clock a number of Officers dined at Patton's Tavern, and then drank the following

"TOASTS.

" '1. THE PATRIOTS OF '76. —May we ever cherish their principles and imitate their virtues.

"2. THE ARMIES OF THE UNITED STATES. —The laurels acquired by them in honorable war have never been sullied by outrages like those of our enemies at Hampton and Frenchtown.

"3. OUR DECLARATION OF INDEPENDENCE. —A beacon to the friends of liberty and a terror to monarchs.

"4. INDEPENDENCE. —May we not lose its substance and court its shadow.

"5. THE NEXT CONGRESS. —May they encourage Domestic Manufacturers and be contented with forty-two dollars a week.

"6. THE LEGISLATIVE AND EXECUTIVE DEPARTMENTS OF THE UNITED STATES. —May they think less about the next Presidency, and more of our National concern.

"7. THE AMERICAN FAIR. —Their smiles animate the soldier's bosom; their virtues awe him into respect.

"A prayer by the Chaplain of the First Regiment followed, then a volley of gunshot from the Common, and the dinner commenced."

Election Day was possibly the loudest and least religious of early American holidays. Although an election sermon was supposed to start the day off, the sermon was most often about the evils of the day, and warnings about the use of election beer. Our present Election Day is strangely mixed up with Guy Fawkes' Day which was observed for many years in America by the burning of bonfires and with parades of children in fantastic costume. In Newburyport, Massachusetts, and Portsmouth, New Hampshire, Guy Fawkes' Day is still recalled. In New York and Brooklyn, the bonfires on the night of election are descendant of those for Guy Fawkes' Day. Fires are still lit on November 5th by some of the back-country children, although they do not know why.

Holidays were once signals to get away from the farm and come to town. Now holidays are times for getting away from the city and rushing to the country. Unfortunately we seem to have less time for one-day enjoyment and relaxation than people used to; even in ox-cart days a ride to town took less time than a present-day trip to the country on a traffic-filled highway often does.

Going to town was once a pleasing experience to the eye when villages were nestled comfortably in valleys and the outskirts were unmarked by road stands and advertising. There was a turn in the road, it always seemed, where the town suddenly came into view. Now roads are straighter and the pattern of the town spills over into the highway for miles before you come to it.

The twisting of old roads was usually intentional. Horses (and humans, too) found "the longest way 'round the sweetest way home" because it eliminated hills. We now go in a straight line up and over hills, whereas we used to

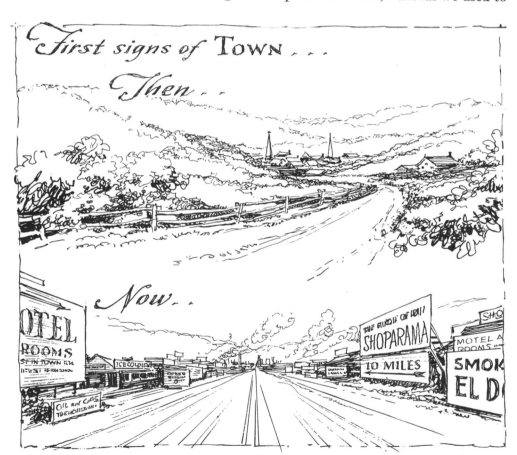

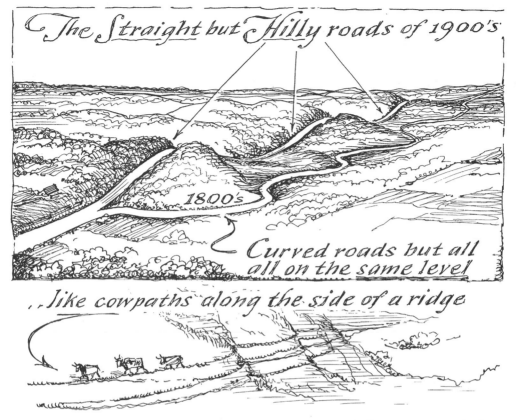

The Straight but Hilly roads of 1900's

1800's

Curved roads but all all on the same level

..like cowpaths along the side of a ridge

keep on the same level and wind around them in much the same manner that a cow travels on a hilly farm.

One of the outstanding changes occurring in small towns during the last few years is the healthy tendency to abandon valleys and move to higher levels. Actually, most cities are built around the principles of two centuries ago, with electrically run mills still crowded over ancient river-powered mill sites. Even regular and devastating floods have not discouraged this practice or persuaded the mill owners to give up their real estate and move to higher ground. Only within the last two decades have highways by-passed valley towns and has small industry built with highway philosophy, avoiding rivers and valleys and floods.

Actually, valley locations are damper and less adaptable to many industries, as well as being areas in which heavier cold air from the hills gravitates and collects. Pollen and smoke and smog, such as you will see over many low-lying industrial cities, likewise settle in the valleys.

One of the greatest differences between the town of the past and the

81

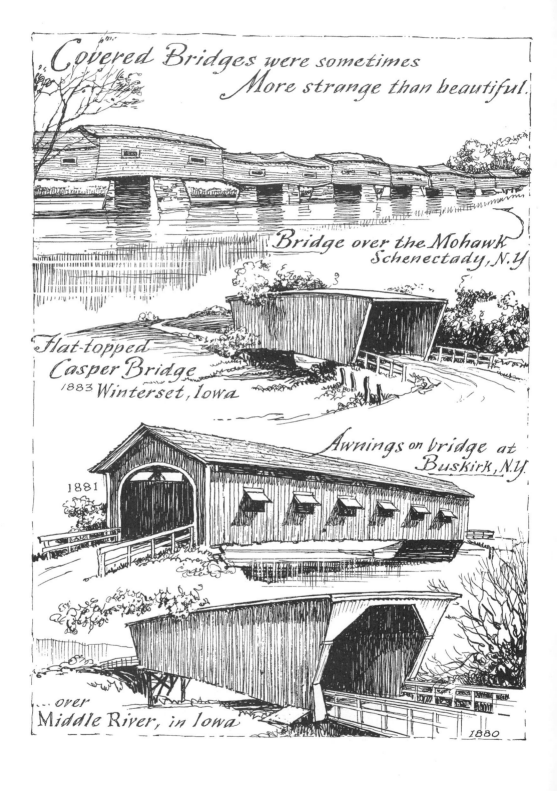

"Covered Bridges were sometimes More strange than beautiful.

Bridge over the Mohawk Schenectady, N.Y.

Flat-topped Casper Bridge 1883 Winterset, Iowa

Awnings on bridge at Buskirk, N.Y.

1881

...over Middle River, in Iowa

1880

city of today is to be found in the atmosphere. The sky seems of limitless height, yet the truth is that one-half of all the atmosphere above sea level lies below a height of 18,000 feet. The average "settling area" of quiet city air is below a thousand feet. Although we are so used to it that we do not notice it, you will actually see the settling level of dirty atmosphere when you fly from a big city airport and almost immediately climb into clear air. New York receives an airborne layer of a half ton of dirt on some city blocks each month. Chicago reported an average of 71.6 tons of dust and dirt on each square mile per month. Sending thirty million tons of soft coal a year into the atmosphere, Chicago finds that most of its dirt is soot, but any big city has the same sewer in its sky, no matter what the character of the foreign matter happens to be. Recently an epidemic of "disintegrating" nylon stockings occurred in major cities, and the phenomenon was found to be caused by "coal and oil in combination with an oxidizing agent within polluted city air"—the same air, of course, that the nylon-wearers inhaled. Some of the chemicals in city air are known to cause cancer in experimental animals, but what we can't see doesn't worry us, so we are mostly concerned with the dirt that rims our shirt collars and makes city apartments dingy.

Never to be left out of the early American picture are the wooden bridges that led to town. Only the covered ones seem to be revered and "collected" by antiquarians, but the uncovered ones were of equal importance.

America's covered bridges are known by the few examples remaining. Those are the ones which were built soundly and which have therefore withstood the ravages of age and the strain of ice floods. But the uncovered bridges which have disappeared or even those which lasted perhaps for only a few months were often as interesting as the longer-lived covered structures.

The idea of collecting a dollar a foot royalty on your own bridge patent became a delightful and fashionable inspiration to all retired men of the 1800's with architectural leanings. By simply adding a brace here or an arch there to your neighbor's patent, you were in business with your own design. Printing houses were soon kept busy making posters and leaflets extolling the virtues of new bridge designs, and men who thought they were destined to the easy chair of old age were suddenly traveling as far as Europe with patented designs for "American-type" wooden bridges. But not everyone could be a Town or a Burr, and many a strange new creation of trestles and arches fell into the river when the builder's scaffold chocks were knocked out.

The number of covered bridges which were carried away during floods, **83** yet were floated back and put into place again, is astonishing. Some were even set on new supports where they came to rest downstream and the road itself

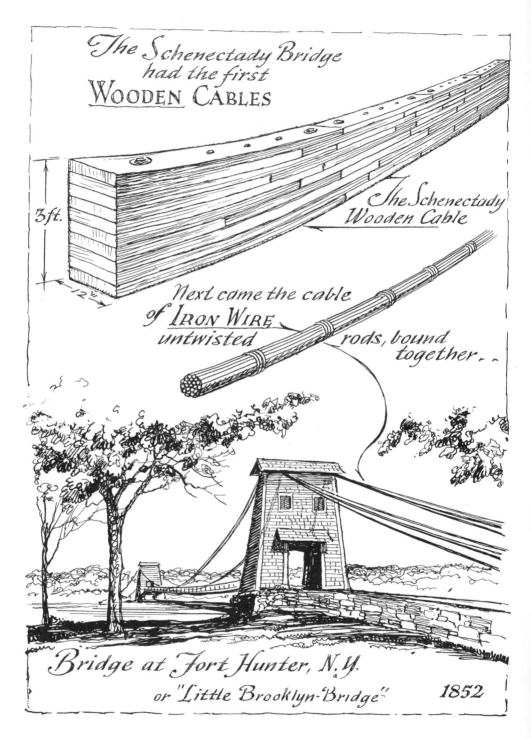

The Schenectady Bridge had the first WOODEN CABLES

3 ft.

12"

The Schenectady Wooden Cable

Next came the cable of IRON WIRE untwisted rods, bound together..

Bridge at Fort Hunter, N.Y. or "Little Brooklyn-Bridge"

1852

was changed to suit their new location. After any good flood, most of the old covered bridges acquired new addresses. There are even records of capsized bridges, the upturned sidewalls of which were used as roadways until a new bridge was built.

America's first suspension bridges were made of rope and chain, as early as 1801, but they were only experimental foot bridges. In 1816 the first wire suspension bridge, using two cables of only three wires each, was thrown across the Schuylkill River at Fairmount in Philadelphia. The wires were only three-eighths of an inch thick and they supported an eighteen-inch foot-path of pine. Stretched four hundred and eight feet between some trees and the upper windows of a wire mill on the other side of the river, it was built

Poster from an old Bridge.

RATES OF
TOLL.

Every Foot Passenger,	3
Every head of live Sheep, Hogs or Calves.	$1\frac{1}{2}$
Every head of Horned Cattle.	9
Every Horse, Jack, Mule or Ox, whether led or drove,	9
Every Horse or Mule and rider,	$12\frac{1}{2}$
Every two wheel Pleasure Carriage, drawn by one Horse, Jack, Mule, and SIX CENTS for every additional Horse, Jack or Mule.	$18\frac{3}{4}$
Every four wheel Pleasure Carriage, the body whereof is supported by springs or thorough-braces, drawn by one Horse, Jack or Mule, and TWELVE AND A HALF CENTS for every additional Horse, Jack or Mule.	25
Every Pleasure Wagon, drawn by one Horse, Jack or Mule, and TWELVE AND A HALF CENTS for every additional Horse, Jack or Mule.	25
Every Stage Wagon, drawn by one Horse, Jack or Mule, and SIX AND A QUARTER CENTS for every additional 3d or 4th Horse, Jack or Mule.	$18\frac{3}{4}$
Every Stage Wagon, drawn by five Horses, Jacks or Mules, and TWENTY-FIVE CENTS for every further additional Horse, Jack or Mule.	37
Every Freight or Burthen Wagon, drawn by one Horse, Jack, Mule or Ox, and SIX CENTS for every additional 3d, 4th or 5th Horse, Jack, Mule or Ox. And for every further additional Horse, Jack, Mule or Ox, TWENTY-FIVE CENTS.	$12\frac{1}{2}$
Every Cart or other two wheel Carriage of burthen, drawn by one Horse, Jack, Mule or Ox, and SIX AND A QUARTER CENTS for every additional Horse, Jack, Mule or Ox.	$12\frac{1}{2}$
Every Sleigh or Sled, of any description, drawn by one Horse, Jack, Mule or Ox, and SIX AND A QUARTER CENTS for every additional Horse, Jack, Mule or Ox.	$12\frac{1}{2}$

Jericho Mill, Vt.

"..when mills were delights to the eye."

in about two weeks. At a toll of one cent per person, it had almost paid for itself within a year, but it collapsed during the first ice storm and was soon forgotten.

Bridge-builder Burr erected a suspension bridge at Schenectady, using great wooden cables one foot wide and three feet high. These spans were no architectural gems, being odd lengths of 160, 190, 180, and 157 feet each. Originally there were three piers in the river to link the four spans but later, when the spans sagged, an extra pier was added under each span, adding to the irregularities. Finally the narrow shingled roofs over each cable were abandoned for a complete bridge housing of hemlock boards, making it one of America's most unique and wavy covered bridges, as shown in the drawing. Although the bridge was unlike any other in America, its toll rates were typically complicated. The list as shown on the opposite page would be enough to drive a modern toll collector mad; between the varying tolls and fines, a bookkeeper and mathematician would have been better suited for the job.

Although the Ramshackle Bridge (as it later came to be known) ended its career dilapidated and uneven, it was once hailed as being "unsurpassed in beauty by any structure in America." It lasted sixty-five years and when it was taken down in 1874 to be sold to a match manufacturer, the massive wooden cables were in perfect condition.

The first metal-cable suspension bridge at Fort Hunter, New York was a Roebling creation of rods or wires lying side by side and bound together. It was supposed to be a small model for the Brooklyn Bridge, and was more an experiment than a finished design. When you walked over it, the floor "came up to meet your feet." In the mildest wind it swayed as much as four feet, and under a fair load it sagged by about the same amount! Between the sway and the sag, many a horse and wagon found itself trapped in the middle and needed a towline and pull to "climb the hill" and reach the other end of the bridge.

Yesterday our city waterfronts were preserved as spots of beauty, but today bridges and docks are often areas of the greatest squalor and evil odors. The country mill and riverside business building were once delights to the eye. However, our consolation lies in the fact that man finds it more difficult to change water areas; rivers and inlets may be less clear, but they still exhibit the same anatomy they possessed a century ago.

Man's inhumanity to the land reaches its peak, it seems, in America's giant sand and gravel pits. Some of them are so permanent and huge that they have become landmarks on aviation maps. Usually near valuable waterfront or along approaches to a city, these scars on the landscape have become "typically American." Zoning boards are usually helpless to bar them because courts have ruled that the sand and gravel business is "farming" and have affirmed the right of any landowner "to remove earth from his own property." Obviously, however, a business which destroys farming and removes the farm itself is not really farming. Today's concrete world needs sand and gravel, but we stand in great need of laws forcing people to level off mining activities when they are finished, so that a worthless scar will not be the heritage of the future landscape.

The word "street" immediately characterizes the city. Originally it had nothing to do with road surface; it measured the distance between two rows of houses. In 1656, when New Amsterdam had one hundred and twenty houses, streets were ordered set off and laid out with stakes, but these streets were measurements without names. Within two years, however, New Amsterdam gave America its first named streets, many of which have now been duplicated in almost every town across the country. It was William Penn who chose a system of naming streets in accordance with the Quaker love of botany, and Philadelphia streets were once almost entirely named from "things that spontaneously grow in the country." Because the early American was familiar with Latin and with the scientific names of plants, some of the old Philadelphia streets became tongue-twisters which it became necessary to change. But enough botanically named streets remain to make intelligible the famous rhyme for remembering their order:

"Market, Arch, Race and Vine,
Chestnut, Walnut, Spruce and Pine."

Streets were often named after some tavern which has long since been forgotten. A great many American towns with strange names were named after an inn famous in the neighborhood. Inns were named for some emblem that could be painted on a signboard and well-preserved in a traveler's memory. Such Pennsylvania towns as Blue Ball, Cross Anchor, Rising Sun, Bird-in-Hand, Broad Axe, King of Prussia, Red Lion, and White Horse often set people speculating as to how their names originated, and what appropriate names they are, at least for a local tavern. Therein, of course, lies the answer.

In 1819 an Act of Congress formally established the Territory of Arkansaw. It was William Woodruff, a Long Island printer, who rebelled against the word Arkansaw. He set up a newspaper press in Arkansaw and reprinted the Act of Congress, changing the name of the new territory to Arkansas. The population of the territory was only about ten thousand, and a great many could not spell, anyway, so Woodruff's version was immediately accepted. Nevertheless, confusion followed, particularly in Kansas and Arkansas City. To this day, although Webster says it should be pronounced "Arkan*so*" and many Kansas people have their own ideas, most people prefer the original form of pronunciation.

Pronunciation was a lesser worry to hundreds of American towns with such strange and unexplainable names as Igo, Peanut, Intercourse, Goodnight, Lovelady, Ticklenaked, Skunk's Misery, and so on. Some continue with their baffling titles; a few have changed their names. But if you want to know the origin of one of these rollicking American town names, and you are certain that it is not derived from the Indian, you will most often find a tavern behind it all, and a sign painter not far away.

Many apparently meaningless names on the ancient taverns were corruptions of familiar phrases of the day, often perpetuated by the successive mistakes of sign painters. The "Pig and Carrot" was originally the "Pique and Carreau"—the spade and diamond of playing cards. A familiar north country tavern name was the "Bell Savage" and the tavern sign usually showed an Indian alongside a large bell. Actually this was a corruption of a popular French book character of the day, a beautiful woman found in the wilderness and called "La Belle Sauvage." "The Bag O' Nails" was originally "The Bacchanalians"; the "Cat and Wheel" was "St. Catherine's Wheel." The "Goat and Compass" came from the motto on an ancient bar, "God encompasseth us." Sign painters renamed many an American town or tavern either by wit or by misspelling.

The American passion for unique advertising signs is no new one. There were slat signs of tavern days that read two different messages, tin signs cut to hammer on covered-bridge rafters, signs cut to put on stair risers, signs with actual animal heads or horns attached to them, even very fat men who were paid to stand outside restaurants with "I Eat Here" signs on their hats or depending from cords about their necks.

Some of the richest American street names live only in people's minds. They are permanent because they are not on the map and therefore cannot be stricken from it. Hell's Kitchen, Back Bay, The Gas House District, The Loop, Harlem, Chinatown, and thousands of others will live on long after the place has changed character entirely. Like the great men of the past, their names remain long after all else has vanished.

People were once required to clean the streets within a certain radius of their own homes. But Benjamin Franklin, who was responsible for so many "firsts" in America, hired the first street cleaner. "After some inquiry," he reported to the Philadelphia Assembly, "I found a poor industrious man who was willing to undertake keeping the pavement clean by sweeping it twice a

Signs

PRATTS BITTERS *for the* KIDNEYS   Ext

DR. BLACKMAN'S GOLDEN EXTRACT 5

PECKS FAMOUS INDIAN RHEUMATIC BALM

OLD FAITHFUL KIDNEY BALM FOR

.. cut to fit Bridge Beams ...

public stairways

...'s Hats

...RICK   SUGAR COATED PILLS

C. HAYRES   HATS SHOES

Pears SOAP

...ntis   BOOK SHO

CUT PLUG   CHIEF BIG BEAR   THE CURE FOR WORN

SMOKE CAINS   SMITHS GUM BALM

Slat signs
that had two
messages

and
fences

1. 2.

HUTTS STORE
20 MILES

COME AGAIN
TO HUTTS

Going   Coming

week, carrying off the dirt from before the neighbor's doors, for the sum of six pence per month, to be paid by each house." Franklin's bill for this first street-cleaning service was put through in 1757. The barrels carried on cart-wheels remained identical in design until they disappeared about twenty years ago, along with the famous city "white wings" or street sweepers.

Street sweepers did not disappear from the big cities only because horses vanished; they faded away mostly because of the congested automobile traffic. European towns still find good use for street sweepers; Russia has all-women crews working on twenty-four-hour shifts, still wielding hand-made twig-and-stick brooms.

Street cleaners and Water wagons . . .

1800

The first lord of the street was the Town Crier. He was also the lamp-lighter. In town-crying days, street lights were bunches of burning pine knots held in an iron cage and suspended from a pole. These had to be fed with fresh pine throughout the night, and it was the town crier's work to do this. The lamplighter of romantic memory and song was a later American of the gas-light era. The writer of this book does not regard himself as ancient, yet he can recall lamplighters in New York City. He likewise recalls that it was they who also delivered the evening paper.

"Extra-boys" are still used in some towns when special news breaks, but they, too, have all but vanished. Fifty years ago their calls of "Wuxtra, read-

PINE-KNOT CAGE
the first
American
Street Light
1650

all-about-it!" was as commonplace as the clang of trolley bells. Things change quickly in the big city.

Early newspapers were folded into four pages, but consisted of one sheet. This was somewhat for convenience, but primarily because the postal laws demanded extra postage for each extra sheet of paper. Before envelopes came into use, letters, for instance, were written on single sheets, folded over and sealed, and sent for one stamp. A letter of two pages would legally require double postage, and newspapers were dealt with in the same manner. A few publishers came out with "bedsheet papers" that were nearly twice ordinary size; when unfolded, they were the size of a full bedsheet.

The old-time newspapers look different and seem inadequate by comparison with those we enjoy today. Yet few of us consider that the readers of those times could have been equally different, and that a twentieth-century paper would not have fitted into the eighteenth-century picture at all. In going through old attics, one will often find trunks full of old newspapers. That in itself is not unusual, but the fact that they are usually complete day-by-day collections for a year at a time should make one reflect. You will seldom hear of anyone outside of the public library keeping such files today. Why did the old-timers do it?

Of course, if we saved our daily papers we would be collecting more advertising matter than news. It seems regrettable that the life of a newspaper now depends upon paid advertising to such an extent that many small-town newspapers must gather news for the main purpose of creating an advertising medium. A New England publisher jokingly commented that "there is so much news in the papers nowadays, you can hardly get around to the ads."

The greatest change in newspaper stalls lies in the array of magazines added to them. Despite the good publications, most of the space is often taken up by "girly" magazines. These cheap publications are attacked by righteous moderns as "endangering our youth." Great-grandfather would not only have spanked his children for reading them, but would have personally chastised the publisher. In looking back at great-grandfather, we realize that his moral indignation was not always an emotion derived from prudishness.

Great-grandfather, it seems, regarded his town in very much the same light as he regarded his own home. The public square with its bandstand and benches and horse foundations had all the furniture of friendliness. Only a mean man could walk down Main Street in a hurry: for the average person it was slow progress because there were so many friends to stop and chat with.

93

Great-grandfather's Occupations

NOT LONG AGO, when a man's work gave him some certain aura, you could guess almost any American's profession simply by looking at him. Now that has become nearly impossible. Air pilots fly in business suits, farmers wear sport coats to town, and actors at last look like any other normal person. The uniform of one's occupation has become lost in present-day regimentation. It seems a pity, too, for there are yet those who are so proud of their occupations that they would still enjoy being identified with them by dress.

The uniforms of occupation are not the only thing that has vanished from the business world: many standard American professions have become obsolete. Trying to recall some, you might think of a few picturesque occupations like stagecoach driving or chimney-sweeping or town-crying. On the contrary, there were hundreds or thousands of major jobs which once occupied a goodly portion of the nation and which are now gone for all time.

Even within the past decade, hundreds of callings became obsolete. Even in the modern world of aviation, hardly a year goes by without witnessing the disappearance of some occupation. One of the most picturesque and American characters was the aviation barnstormer, whom we might pass by as an unimportant worker. Actually, there have been about five thousand professional barnstormers in America and their work was more important than even they dreamed.

After the First World War, when the airplane was regarded as nothing

94

more than a novel piece of war machinery, thousands of men returned to civilian life with the roar of motors still in their ears. With uncrated surplus OX-5 and Hispano-Suiza engines selling for two hundred dollars apiece, who could resist the temptation to build his own ship or buy an old Army "Jenny"?

For the next twenty years the country was treated to "air circuses" and passenger flights wherever there was an empty field and enough people to pay. The barnstorming birdman was born; wearing his cap backward, high laced boots, waxed moustache, and a scarf that trailed out behind him when in flight, he made a dashing picture, indeed. At night he often had to sleep in the field under the plane's wing, but by day he was the hero of young America.

Many people still recall the Gates Flying Circus and their method of advertising their show. When the group came to town, they unloosed rolls of toilet paper, which floated gaily across the sky and finally festooned trees and buildings, to tell the populace that an air show was to be seen at the fair grounds. With Gates there was always a special daredevil known as "Diavolo," who walked wings and actually stood atop the upper wing while the

Birdman 1920

95

plane looped. As each Diavolo finally plunged to his death, a new one took the name. Pilot "Duke" Kranz, who was the last Diavolo, is still active in the aviation world at the time of this writing.

The average barnstormer was regarded as a foolish daredevil, drunk much of the time. The poor fellow had sold his home and belongings to buy his plane and keep it in repair, and he inevitably sold his life in the bargain. Very few people realized that he was doing important work which the military forces should have undertaken at government expense. When the last great air show ended at Cleveland, Ohio in 1939, the souped-up motors and improvised plane designs for which the five thousand barnstormers had footed the bills were our most valuable military asset. They had reached a stage at which they could do little to make their ships go faster except saw a few inches off their wings each race day, and by then wings the length of ironing boards were lifting the nation's heaviest stock engines into the air. Those "crazy air devils" deserve a place in the nation's respect which has never been accorded them. And a military salute, too, for they are among the greatest of America's unsung heroes.

One of the quickest disappearances of any big business was that of the American natural-ice industry. Just fifty years ago there were some ten thou-

... a few inches off the wings each year

1939

sand men in America cutting natural ice during the winter months. They were a fabulous race, often farmer boys who found winter on the farm too slow and financially unproductive; others were drifters from river life or the lumber country who depended on picking up a winter's stake. Salaries included room and board, but so many blankets were ripped up and used for foot wrappings and warm undergarments that ice cutters were usually instructed to bring their own bedding.

Today, no record of the ice cutters, except an occasional anecdote about their rough living, survives. The icehouses in which they worked have vanished. Only a foundation or an abandoned railroad track marks their locations, but almost every pond and lake will produce some evidence of their existence. Icehouses were sometimes so big that clouds formed and rain fell within them. Often the railroad's busiest tracks were the ones which serviced the icehouses. The electric switch that starts your refrigerator machinery in less than five years blasted forever one of America's major industries and sent the ice cutter into an oblivion of Americana.

The first icehouses were farm root cellars. Pennsylvania farmers used to shovel snow and ice into their root cellars just before the thaw of spring; they found that, by packing a little meadow grass with it, the ice could be made to last into the next summer. By 1830 icehouses were standard farm equipment. The usual procedure was to build them of two walls with hay in between. Virginia icehouses were actually two separate houses, one built inside the other, with enough room in the vacant space for a man to walk. The sides and roof of both "houses" were thatched, and the ice placed in the inner house on a bed of straw.

In 1799 ice was cut from Canal Street in New York City and sent to Charleston, South Carolina by boat; it was welcomed with fife and drum and chopped up in drinks for city officials. It had melted considerably by the time it reached the dock down south, but the experiment was a success and the idea of exporting ice was born. In 1805, a man named Frederic Tudor from Boston sent one hundred and thirty tons of ice in the brig *Favorite* to Martinique in the West Indies. In 1815 he contracted to supply the Cuban government and by 1833 he had contracts with Madras, Bombay, and Calcutta.

To hint at the size of the American natural-ice business as early as 1847, we find Boston records showing 51,887 tons sent to coastal ports and 22,591 tons sent abroad. The returns for that year in Boston were far above the half-million-dollar mark. Multiplying this by the hundreds of other ice businesses, you may see that the industry was a major one for America.

The only evidence of the early ice cutter remaining may be his tools, which were sometimes made in the farm's forge barn. Even the later manu-

1910

*Ice-houses
so big that real clouds
formed inside!*

Ice-cutting at Lake Hopatcong, N.J.

Snow Warden

Snow Paving the road

factured tools are beginning to disappear now: the common ice tongs, ice saw and other paraphernalia of the ice cutter may already be seen in the antique shops. Natural ice for anything except skating will soon be past Americana. Even now we skate largely on artificial ice!

The ice and snow of yesteryear, one might think, should have inconvenienced the farmer, yet winter was a season to which he looked forward! Every hauling job waited for the first snow or ice because only then were the soft and uneven roads of yesterday really usable.

Instead of plowing the snow away as we do today, snow rollers packed it down and everyone traveled on top. One of the town's most important jobs was that of snow warden; he was the man who supervised "road packing" and, oddly enough, was responsible for covering the bare spots with snow. The whole northern country moved by sled in winter, and a bare spot on a snow-covered road became a frustrating roadblock. The snow warden's most tiring job was to "snow-pave" covered bridges so sleds could pass through. This, of course, explodes the theory that bridges were covered to keep them free of snow.

For every wagon a farmer owned, he once had about three sleds. Wheels were more for pleasure or light-carriage transportation: all heavy hauling was postponed until winter and moved over ice and snow. A few farmers improvised detachable runners to put beneath wagon wheels; just before the gasoline truck entered the scene, detachable runners were manufactured and sold by mail-order houses.

One road traveler who was never bothered by weather, good or bad, was the drover. And a most remarkable person he was. When one remembers that a farmer often entrusted his entire year's stock to his care, one realizes how sober and reliable a gentleman the drover must have been. He was also one of the first American advertising men: his pung (sled) was so covered with signs advertising taverns or patent medicines that he seldom needed other identification.

Drovers who walked livestock from the farm to the city often found themselves guardians to a varied group. Cows and sheep and goats were comparatively simple to handle, but geese and turkeys made the drover's life difficult. The drover's dog is a forgotten animal, but it is said that his ability as a herder was amazing. While the drover slept, he depended upon his dog to guard his flock and warn him of any irregularity.

Among the feats of a drover was that of separating large droves into legal limits for crossing toll bridges. There seemed to be a standard fine of a dollar for any drove "of horses, jacks, mules, or oxen more than ten, at a distance less than thirty feet apart" over a wooden bridge. But it is doubted that a drover ever paid the fine, for he was usually the tollbridge keeper's best customer.

Tobacco drovers were the truck drivers of their day for those plantations without a river at their door. The commonest way of delivering tobacco from isolated farms to river docks was by "giant hogshead." This was a tremendous wooden barrel equipped with iron-bound "tire hoops"; a team of horses could pull such a hogshead of tobacco through jungle which no wagon might possibly navigate. Although the idea originated in the deep South, tobacco hogsheads were also common in New England. The hogshead was an old English measure of capacity (63 gallons of wine and 54 gallons of beer), but the American use of the giant hogshead for tobacco transportation enlarged

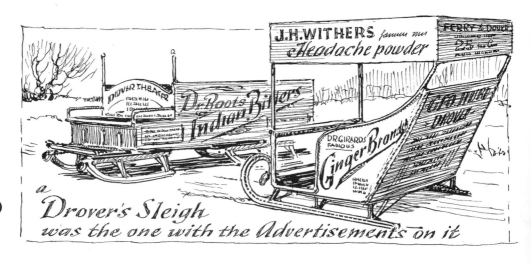

100

a Drover's Sleigh was the one with the Advertisements on it

Tobacco Drovers

-- a Giant Hogshead

its proportions to contain from 750 to 1200 pounds, varying in different states.

The drover had no standard identifying uniform, although many wore wide-brim hats and large capes. A staff to handle the animals was sometimes supplemented by a long pole with a red flag on it so that stagecoach traffic might be warned of an approaching drove. When railroads were young, locomotives had to be "escorted from one end of town to the other"; the town drover had the job of riding ahead on horseback with a red flag. Because that law had never been changed, freight trains moving about on the west side of New York's Manhattan Island were preceded by a man, horse, and red flag until only a few years ago.

The stage driver was more than a driver of horses like the English coachman; he was a power in the land. He carried political news from country to town and he was noted for the great kindness of delivering messages from farmhouse to farmhouse. A toot on the stagecoach horn would bring a farm wife to the door, where the driver might slow his horses to a walk and call out that "Netty had twins and she's doin' good," or other such news. Stagecoach drivers were second to sea captains in many ways and, like men of the sea, usually retired abruptly while their sons continued on the highways, "born to the box."

Children always associated a trip on the stage with an ocean voyage: such, indeed, was the common custom. The driver was referred to as captain, his crew always "got aboard," the inside of the coach was "the cabin," and the top was called "the deck." Most coaches were named after famous ships and

New Hampshire driver
in winter...

3 sets of shoes and
giant "over-stockings"

the summer headgear of drivers was often a sea captain's cap. Few people knew a stagecoach driver's first name and, although his constant imbibing of ale, brandy, and rum-and-milk must have had its effect, his dignity remained great and dominant. Young children were often entrusted to his care, and as soon as the coach had left town, the driver's word was as much law as that of any captain at sea.

The New Hampshire stage driver's winter dress identified him at once. Homespun trousers were tucked inside thin leather boots with fur-lined overshoes over the boots. Over these were worn Canadian hand-knit red stockings coming well up over the knees, creating the appearance of tremendously heavy legs. Incredible as it may seem, another light shoe was added, making three pairs of shoes in all! The driver's coats and caps were fur, and a red silk sash with tassels completed the costume.

Many of the early railroad brakemen, conductors, ticket men, and depot masters were former stage drivers. Benjamin Pierce Cheney, a prominent Boston railroad owner, founder of the rich Cheney Express, and chief owner of the American Express Company, began as a stage driver in New Hampshire between Exeter and Nashua. The rail lines soon had positions open for any stage driver who would accept, and the great American stage driver vanished into the complexities of the railroad business.

Another vanished knight of the road is the old-fashioned peddler whose home and shop was his wagon. He both bought and sold as he went, often selling his stock, horse, wagon, and all. Starting anew, with a few wares on his back, he invariably returned with a new horse and wagon and a tidy profit besides.

"Peddler" and "drummer" are typically American words. The ancient Scotch "peder" or foot-salesman became the "pedlar" of the New World. Although in England "peddlers" traveled only by foot and "hawkers" went only by wagon, anyone who sold wares from door to door in America became commonly known as a peddler. The drummer, or man who went about "drumming up trade," actually stemmed from the earliest time when drums were used to attract public attention, just as when church was called by a drum and public announcements were made after a drum call. The first American peddlers often carried a drum known as a "chapman's drum." The Yankee peddler was known to the townspeople of his time as a "chapman," a word which comes from the Anglo-Saxon "ceap" for trade, plus "man" (hence a "cheap-man"). The chapman who later won fame as a Yankee peddler often carried a drum and an American flag and boasted loudly that he sold only American goods. Actually, it was illegal for him to do otherwise, but he was a good salesman. The Connecticut statutes of the middle

ASK FOR IT: I HAVE IT

The Peddler was an American Farm Institution

eighties said that "any petty-chapman dealing, trading or trafficking in foreign goods which are not the product of the United States, shall have his goods seized. One-half the value of the goods seized shall go to the State and the other half shall go to the informer."

The Yankee peddler was the original American who could "sell anyone anything." One of his claims to fame is his origination of the name "Nutmeg State" for Connecticut; this derived from the belief that the Connecticut peddler sold wooden nutmegs as real ones. Few people, however, know that nutmegs were famous in Connecticut on their own merits. The nutmeg was the most popular flavoring of the old days; it was even favored as a gift. Nutmegs were gilded and ribboned and given as presents, not only because of their worth, but because they were supposed to have great medicinal value. Some of the silver trinkets of colonial days which many people believe are snuff boxes were actually nutmeg-holders. The inside of the cover was often pierced to form a grater and served also as an opening to let the aroma escape. The *bon vivants* and fashionable dames of the period carried nutmegs with them at all times as a sign of luxury. Because nutmegs were valuable and because they were easy to carry, it was always a convenient money-maker for the traveling peddler, who was often called a "nutmeg man."

American rivers have reversed their roles in the American scene during the past century, and with this change a great race of men has vanished. Today, rivers are often obstacles to travel, whereas yesterday they were the main means of inland transportation. At one time it was easier to push a cargo by flatboat with long poles for a few hundred miles than it would be to roll it on wheels over the then impassable roads. Before steam came to propel boats, the entire American river commerce depended upon the strength of river men, the likes of whom we shall never see again. In 1870 William Cullen Bryant wrote: "The keel-boatmen of the Mississippi were a remarkable race. . . . In strength they were absolute giants; in power of sustaining fatigue, without rivals in any age. If they had been classical in their exultation of physical power, they would confidently have challenged Hercules to combat, and, in our opinion, would have conquered that old Greek." The keel-boatmen have long since gone and only by folklore has their remarkable

of thousands of *Keelboats,* not one remains

75' long

River Men . . a race of giants

Grindstone City

The Ghost city of discarded Grindstones

Grindstone set in tree-fork

Water-can on willow-stick.

1860, Bucks County Pa.

size and strength been recorded. Mike Fink is to the river what Davy Crockett has become to the southwest, yet the story now is one of roughness and toughness rather than of the remarkable size and strength required for men actually to push large cargoes from town to town. One of the river stories concerns a giant of a river man who lived on an Ohio flatboat with his family of twelve children. After delivering a load of large grindstones to a pier, he decided to make some extra money and take them directly to the warehouse in town. He carried a stack of them on his back, while each of the children rolled one grindstone down the village street like a hoop.

Incidentally, grindstones as the average person knows them are something else from the past. They are often mistaken for, and are even sold by some antique shops, as millstones. Few old farmhouses have less than a dozen grindstones lying around the grounds or in the barns, but the greatest collection is probably at Grindstone City in Michigan. Buried along the shore there are hundreds of tons of good grindstones, discarded when new-type abrasives were developed.

Grindstones were first imported from England and later from Nova Scotia. America first quarried grindstones in Berea, Ohio, but by 1840 small mills appeared almost everywhere, grinding rock into serviceable grindstones to sell to the farmers. There were once about two hundred villages called Grindstone; only five remain.

The early grindstone man simply sold the stone and let the farmer make his own "grinding horse"; the first ones were turned by hand and therefore required two men to serve as operators. The more recent ones had a foot pedal. You can still buy foot-pedal grindstones, equipped with spring tractor seats, from a few mail-order houses. The first grindstones were placed in the crotch of a forked tree trunk; a can of water on a willow stick wiggled above, as the wheel turned, and splashed on the stone below. The later "grindstone man" was a big-city knife and scissor sharpener who carried his equipment on his back. The sketch of a grindstone man shows him also carrying a large advertising board: when he went into a house to collect knives or scissors, he naturally left his grinding stand outside and the sign told passersby that he was in the neighborhood and open for business.

The most famous "walking signs" were those of the more recent "sandwich men." You may still see sandwich men walking between their two advertising signs, but they are usually derelicts picking up money while otherwise out of work. New York once had agencies which hired groups of sandwich men and the scheme was always a popular part of any local advertising campaign. Restaurants and barber shops are examples of businesses which still employ sandwich men for advertising.

1750 Grindstones were sold unmounted

and made for 2 man operation

"I grind!"

GRIND STONE MAN

CHEAP

1850

The first one-man Grindstone was that of the town Grinder

Sandwich-men 1900

The barber shop of a century ago was not unlike that of today in its lay-out. The chair, however, was without arms and there was a separate stool for the feet. The barber's best advertisement was his array of shaving mugs inscribed with the owners' names. The ordinary customer hid under the ano-nymity of a number, but the town elite were represented by coats of arms, signs of their professions, and various embellishments in color and gold leaf. The whole array was a vivid advertisement of the barber's popularity.

Barber shops used to be museums of bric-a-brac; even today the small-town barber shop will often be filled with exotic plants and curious treasures. This custom stems from the time when the barber was also a surgeon, and the doctor's office was also a museum where stuffed animals were hung from the ceiling, skeletons were propped up in corners, and all sorts of strange things

109

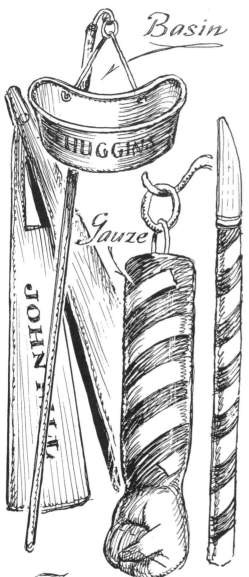

Basin

Gauze

JOHN

Typical
Barber Surgeon
Signs

110

BARBER

The Negro and the
Razor

were to be seen sealed in glass jars. The first street signs of the barber did not advertise his hair-cutting, but rather his profession of blood-letting. The red pole with a spiraled white line represents a bleeding arm wrapped with white gauze. Another such sign was a barber's basin hung from a pole; the same basin used to catch shaving lather also caught blood from a patient who was being bled. The barber-surgeon profession began with a decree in 1092 stating that monks must not wear beards. "Barba-men" (from the Latin word for beard) were trained to shave monks and also to bleed them in time of sickness because their pans and cutting equipment were so similar. Unfortunately, they were often the same.

The earliest mention of barbers in America is in the *Archives* of Pennsylvania for 1702. It reveals that four barbers were fined for trimming people "on the first days of the week." Another early record is that of a Negro barber of Connecticut in 1730 who had no shop but made the rounds of the countryside in a wagon. The association of the Negro and the razor in American folklore has good foundation because until about 1820 Negroes controlled the profession of shaving and hair-cutting. As late as 1884, Chamber's *Encyclopedia of New York* said, "In the United States the business of barbering is almost exclusively in the hands of the colored population."

Typical of the small town was its attitude toward the unfortunate and weak-minded. It never tolerated a drunk, yet every town had its eccentrics who were good-naturedly passed off as "town characters." There is no room now for the hermits, the wanderers, the solitaries, and town do-nothings who were accepted a century ago. New Canaan, Connecticut harbored "Crazy Sam" who came out only after dark, when he yodeled until morning. Westerly, Rhode Island had the "Astronomer" who lived in summer on berries and in winter on nuts and grain; his ability to predict weather was reportedly unexcelled. He seldom showed himself, but he left strange messages scratched upon pumpkins. There were men who just "loathed the nearness of others" and became hermits in caves, in holes in the ground, or retreated into themselves. And great-grandfather tolerated them with the same patience and understanding that he would show to one of his own.

Most renowned of America's eccentrics was possibly Johnny Appleseed, who blamed his strange ways on an unhappy love affair. He was a religious man who wore few clothes and traveled barefoot. He always carried a Bible and a supply of apple seeds with him. On his head he wore a tin pan which he also used for cooking his meals. His real name was Jonathan Chapman and he was just another "touched" person who accepted the hospitality of yesteryear. But the kindness of the towns through which he traveled was more than repaid by his planting of apple seeds. After walking twenty miles

White water men

during one day in 1847, he stopped at the home of friends in Fort Wayne, Indiana to read his Bible to them and leave them the customary supply of seeds. There he died at the age of seventy-two.

You might say that the lumberjack and riverjack are still with us, but even they will be the first to admit that the old-timer at their work was a person entirely different from his modern counterpart. Timber is moved now mostly by rail and truck, but in the old days it was moved by river. Water continues to be a useful method of moving logs, but most log drives are tame ferry operations where the riverjack's work consists only of guiding the logs through calm water. The riverjack was once a "white-water man" who let the apprentice do his calm-water work and saved his acrobatic daring for the dangerous waters of rapids and swift rivers.

The only surviving white-water log drive in the east is still operating on the Machias River in Maine. Other survivors are the annual drives on the Clearwater River in Idaho and the Saguenay in Quebec.

A log drive takes about two weeks, and the moving force of melting snow is a power that is calculated and timed for weeks ahead. A riverjack might drink for the rest of the year, but when spring approached he became a quiet, sure-footed athlete. The old-time white-water man had a short life and he seldom found a wife to share his rugged existence, so the breed has nearly disappeared.

A century ago the riverfront of almost any town was crowded with logs. Each log had a name or initials marked on it and was waiting to be picked up by the owner who might take a month traveling downstream from the point where the log was cut. Of course, there was much argument over the ownership of many logs, and the log-viewer was called in to make his legal decision.

The title of inspector is recent: not long ago the word was "viewer." There were weight-viewers, fence-viewers, egg-viewers, gutter-viewers, and viewers of whatever needed inspection or supervision. Hardly a law was passed without a set of viewers to go along with it. From the beginning, viewers were seldom popular people; as years passed, viewing was embodied in a town ordinance for the resolution of personal disputes, and the government inspector became the "policeman" we know of today. If your neighbor put his fence on what you thought was your property, you called neither the policeman nor the surveyor, but the town fence-viewer. When he was on duty, the fence-viewer usually had two chainmen who carried the "Gunter's Chain" for measuring land distances, and he also worked closely with the hayward. The hayward was the man who impounded stray cattle and fined the owner. The similar words "strayward" and "straywarden" will not be found in the dictionary, but are still used in the Arkansas back country.

Another forgotten word is "wright." Millwright, shipwright, wheelwright, cartwright, and wainwright (wagon-maker) are words that have become people's proper names, but which have all joined the world of vanished occupations. The wheelwright began as an apprentice woodsman and

Settling a dispute.

Perch-pole or rod 16½'

fence-viewer.

Chainman *Gunter's Chain (4 rods or 66 feet long).*

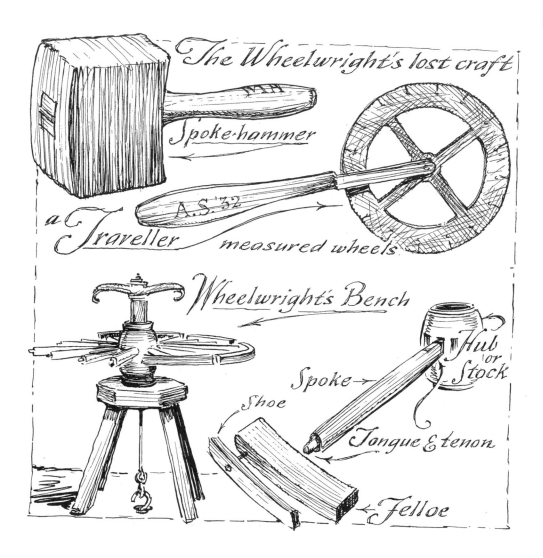

The Wheelwright's lost craft

Spoke-hammer

a Traveller   measured wheels

A.S. '32

Wheelwright's Bench

Spoke →

Shoe

Hub or Stock

Tongue & tenon

Felloe

became America's greatest wood expert. The spidery web of wheel that reached perfection during the Victorian age could not be made again. Its strength improved with age because its properly seasoned woods supplemented each other's merits to weld a unit as close to perfection as man has ever produced. Only well into the nineteenth century did the wheelwright use a circular iron tire; before that the wheel was shod only with strakes or curved sections over each spoke end. That enormous weights could speed over the rough roads of yesterday on wooden wheels much slenderer than modern bicycle tires and without any metal fastenings seems almost miraculous. Black or sour gum for hubs, oak or ash for spokes, hickory for felloes, beech or fresh ash for axles, oak for framing, and poplar for paneling were some of the many combinations of wood that made up a lasting wagon. Such combinations were the "secret recipes" of the old wheelwright, and he made every effort to keep them secret, as he did his methods of seasoning.

There is no need for anything but metal wheels today; when the world moved on dirt roads, however, a fine wooden wheel meant a great deal to the expert and almost every man was an expert. The "feel" and spring, even the sound, of a properly made wheel added to the enjoyment of yesterday's travel. But now all that is gone and wrights are practically extinct. Even the "smiths" who succeeded them in the iron age are on their way to oblivion.

A smith, the derivation of whose name is almost forgotten, is "a man who strikes." The meaning is derived from the word "smite," and the smith's tool was a hammer. Today we know only of the blacksmith and tinsmith. Not long ago, the whitesmith, working in lighter metals, was equally well-known. The blacksmith's shop, with doors open during the summer and a comfortably warm fire in winter, offered the country men a receptive atmosphere for gathering and gossip. The blacksmith ranked with the cobbler as a rural philosopher, but his hammer had more emphasis and the "mighty smith" became the greater legend.

The early farms all had their own forge barns, and it was almost unheard of for a farmer to have his horse's shoes made to order by a town blacksmith. The blacksmith's work was that of making such fine metal parts as hinges, guns, pots, or machinery. Only in later years, when specialization came into being and the gunsmith, the hingesmith, the tinsmith and other specialists opened their shops, did the blacksmith's art deteriorate to horseshoe making and the general rough farm smithing which we associate with the "village smithy."

In 1717 Jonathan Dickinson wrote: "This last summer one Thomas **115** Rutter, a smith who lives not far from Germantown, hath removed further up in the country, and of his own strength has set upon making iron." From

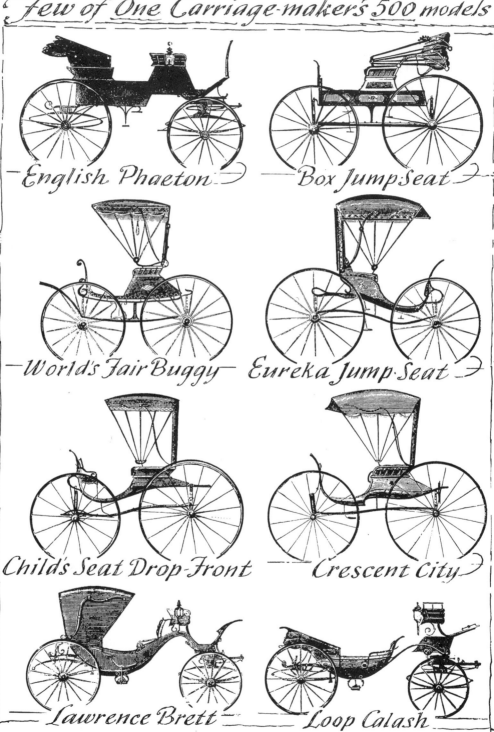

A Few of One Carriage-maker's 500 models

English Phaeton

Box Jump Seat

World's Fair Buggy

Eureka Jump-Seat

Child's Seat Drop-Front

Crescent City

Lawrence Brett

Loop Calash

Doctor's Phaeton

Full top Cabriolet

Champion

Prince of Wales

Dayton Brett

City Coupe

Brewster Calash Coach

Coupe Rockaway

that early date, a number of German blacksmiths devoted a part of their time to mining and smelting iron in their own furnaces. Ore was melted in stone stacks about twenty feet high, often built by one man and standing undamaged today after two hundred years. The furnace was built into the side of a hill so that the ore, charcoal, and limestone could be hauled to the top by oxen and dumped into the stack. The process went on continually day and night for about nine months of the year.

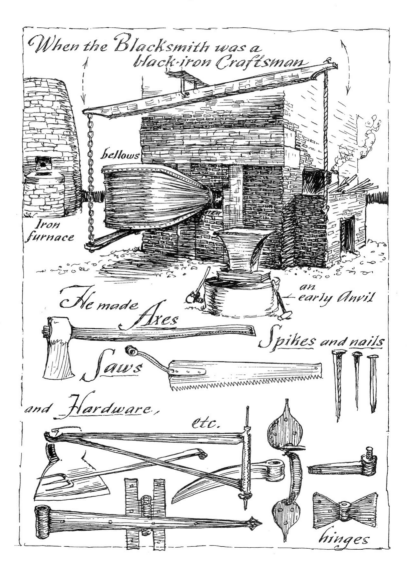

When the Blacksmith was a black-iron Craftsman

bellows

Iron furnace

He made Axes

an early Anvil

Spikes and nails

Saws

and Hardware,

etc.

hinges

The amount of charcoal used to smelt iron was staggering, but the amount of wood used to make the charcoal was almost beyond comprehension. In 1840 the small town of Salisbury, Connecticut was using five thousand cords of wood a year in the manufacture of iron. This amount is hardly more than a mathematical figure, but if you visualize it in the form of one pile of wood in cord-width (4' x 4'), such a woodpile would be over seven miles long. This, multiplied by the hundreds of iron-producing towns of that time, made a pitiful gap in the forests of America and cleared the farmer's countryside of every available tree.

When coke took over the work of charcoal, about ten thousand charcoal workers were left to find other employment. They were mostly Europeans who could speak no English and whose life of seclusion with their lonely charcoal stacks had turned them into a strange race of hermits. Like the others engaged in lost occupations, they had a rich history and suffered a sad disappearance.

With all the vanished occupations, a good deal of American tradition was shelved, for a man's work is reflected in his thinking as much as his thinking is reflected in his work. Great-grandfather not only built a business for his sons, but enjoyed evolving a philosophy to go with it and bestowed that upon his offspring as well. The inheritance of a principle, however, is like the inheritance of money: it needs constant and wise application lest it become lost.

Occupations are born quickly today and often die without achieving stature and character. It is then that a worker comes to resemble a discarded machine with nothing in the nature of business to leave to his children except money. The American heritage too frequently consists of nothing else.

His individuality, his church, his home, his town, and his occupation were the things great-grandfather most enjoyed bestowing. These things, he knew, were the ingredients of freedom. But freedom, while a heritage, must be rewon for each generation. These things were known to the American yesterday.

Fed by hand-cart

Chimney

Stack

bosh

hearth

to Bellows
operated by a
Water Wheel

Ruins of an early Furnace

120

Charcoal Burners often lived like solitary Animals

..in Sod·huts similar to their Charcoal Mounds

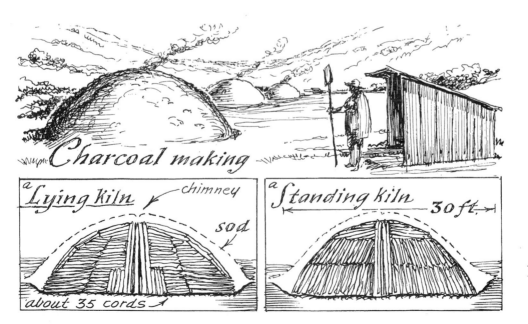

Charcoal making

a *Lying kiln* — chimney

sod

about 35 cords

a *Standing kiln* — 30 ft.

Postscript

THERE IS NO PLACE for nostalgia in a progressive world. The new school not only ignores nostalgia, but condemns it. The world of yesterday is becoming an isolated world of remembrances and echoes so forbidden that, to decorate the present with it, you must often do so with a sense of humor or belong to a select group. If this book is pessimistic about the present, and not merely enthusiastic about some of the past, then I have missed my objective. But such is the chance an individualist inevitably runs.

ERIC SLOANE

A CATALOG OF SELECTED DOVER
BOOKS IN ALL FIELDS OF INTEREST

CONCERNING THE SPIRITUAL IN ART, Wassily Kandinsky. Pioneering work by father of abstract art. Thoughts on color theory, nature of art. Analysis of earlier masters. 12 illustrations. 80pp. of text. 5⅜ x 8½. 0-486-23411-8

CELTIC ART: The Methods of Construction, George Bain. Simple geometric techniques for making Celtic interlacements, spirals, Kells-type initials, animals, humans, etc. Over 500 illustrations. 160pp. 9 x 12. (Available in U.S. only.) 0-486-22923-8

AN ATLAS OF ANATOMY FOR ARTISTS, Fritz Schider. Most thorough reference work on art anatomy in the world. Hundreds of illustrations, including selections from works by Vesalius, Leonardo, Goya, Ingres, Michelangelo, others. 593 illustrations. 192pp. 7⅛ x 10¼. 0-486-20241-0

CELTIC HAND STROKE-BY-STROKE (Irish Half-Uncial from "The Book of Kells"): An Arthur Baker Calligraphy Manual, Arthur Baker. Complete guide to creating each letter of the alphabet in distinctive Celtic manner. Covers hand position, strokes, pens, inks, paper, more. Illustrated. 48pp. 8¼ x 11. 0-486-24336-2

EASY ORIGAMI, John Montroll. Charming collection of 32 projects (hat, cup, pelican, piano, swan, many more) specially designed for the novice origami hobbyist. Clearly illustrated easy-to-follow instructions insure that even beginning papercrafters will achieve successful results. 48pp. 8¼ x 11. 0-486-27298-2

BLOOMINGDALE'S ILLUSTRATED 1886 CATALOG: Fashions, Dry Goods and Housewares, Bloomingdale Brothers. Famed merchants' extremely rare catalog depicting about 1,700 products: clothing, housewares, firearms, dry goods, jewelry, more. Invaluable for dating, identifying vintage items. Also, copyright-free graphics for artists, designers. Co-published with Henry Ford Museum & Greenfield Village. 160pp. 8¼ x 11. 0-486-25780-0

THE ART OF WORLDLY WISDOM, Baltasar Gracian. "Think with the few and speak with the many," "Friends are a second existence," and "Be able to forget" are among this 1637 volume's 300 pithy maxims. A perfect source of mental and spiritual refreshment, it can be opened at random and appreciated either in brief or at length. 128pp. 5⅜ x 8½. 0-486-44034-6

JOHNSON'S DICTIONARY: A Modern Selection, Samuel Johnson (E. L. McAdam and George Milne, eds.). This modern version reduces the original 1755 edition's 2,300 pages of definitions and literary examples to a more manageable length, retaining the verbal pleasure and historical curiosity of the original. 480pp. 5⁵⁄₁₆ x 8¼. 0-486-44089-3

ADVENTURES OF HUCKLEBERRY FINN, Mark Twain, Illustrated by E. W. Kemble. A work of eternal richness and complexity, a source of ongoing critical debate, and a literary landmark, Twain's 1885 masterpiece about a barefoot boy's journey of self-discovery has enthralled readers around the world. This handsome clothbound reproduction of the first edition features all 174 of the original black-and-white illustrations. 368pp. 5⅜ x 8½. 0-486-44322-1

FRENCH STORIES/CONTES FRANÇAIS: A Dual-Language Book, Wallace Fowlie. Ten stories by French masters, Voltaire to Camus: "Micromegas" by Voltaire; "The Atheist's Mass" by Balzac; "Minuet" by de Maupassant; "The Guest" by Camus, six more. Excellent English translations on facing pages. Also French-English vocabulary list, exercises, more. 352pp. 5⅜ x 8½. 0-486-26443-2

CHICAGO AT THE TURN OF THE CENTURY IN PHOTOGRAPHS: 122 Historic Views from the Collections of the Chicago Historical Society, Larry A. Viskochil. Rare large-format prints offer detailed views of City Hall, State Street, the Loop, Hull House, Union Station, many other landmarks, circa 1904-1913. Introduction. Captions. Maps. 144pp. 9⅜ x 12¼. 0-486-24656-6

OLD BROOKLYN IN EARLY PHOTOGRAPHS, 1865-1929, William Lee Younger. Luna Park, Gravesend race track, construction of Grand Army Plaza, moving of Hotel Brighton, etc. 157 previously unpublished photographs. 165pp. 8⅞ x 11¾. 0-486-23587-4

THE MYTHS OF THE NORTH AMERICAN INDIANS, Lewis Spence. Rich anthology of the myths and legends of the Algonquins, Iroquois, Pawnees and Sioux, prefaced by an extensive historical and ethnological commentary. 36 illustrations. 480pp. 5⅜ x 8½. 0-486-25967-6

AN ENCYCLOPEDIA OF BATTLES: Accounts of Over 1,560 Battles from 1479 B.C. to the Present, David Eggenberger. Essential details of every major battle in recorded history from the first battle of Megiddo in 1479 B.C. to Grenada in 1984. List of Battle Maps. New Appendix covering the years 1967-1984. Index. 99 illustrations. 544pp. 6½ x 9¼. 0-486-24913-1

SAILING ALONE AROUND THE WORLD, Captain Joshua Slocum. First man to sail around the world, alone, in small boat. One of great feats of seamanship told in delightful manner. 67 illustrations. 294pp. 5⅜ x 8½. 0-486-20326-3

ANARCHISM AND OTHER ESSAYS, Emma Goldman. Powerful, penetrating, prophetic essays on direct action, role of minorities, prison reform, puritan hypocrisy, violence, etc. 271pp. 5⅜ x 8½. 0-486-22484-8

MYTHS OF THE HINDUS AND BUDDHISTS, Ananda K. Coomaraswamy and Sister Nivedita. Great stories of the epics; deeds of Krishna, Shiva, taken from puranas, Vedas, folk tales; etc. 32 illustrations. 400pp. 5⅜ x 8½. 0-486-21759-0

MY BONDAGE AND MY FREEDOM, Frederick Douglass. Born a slave, Douglass became outspoken force in antislavery movement. The best of Douglass' autobiographies. Graphic description of slave life. 464pp. 5⅜ x 8½. 0-486-22457-0

FOLLOWING THE EQUATOR: A Journey Around the World, Mark Twain. Fascinating humorous account of 1897 voyage to Hawaii, Australia, India, New Zealand, etc. Ironic, bemused reports on peoples, customs, climate, flora and fauna, politics, much more. 197 illustrations. 720pp. 5⅜ x 8½. 0-486-26113-1

THE PEOPLE CALLED SHAKERS, Edward D. Andrews. Definitive study of Shakers: origins, beliefs, practices, dances, social organization, furniture and crafts, etc. 33 illustrations. 351pp. 5⅜ x 8½. 0-486-21081-2

THE MYTHS OF GREECE AND ROME, H. A. Guerber. A classic of mythology, generously illustrated, long prized for its simple, graphic, accurate retelling of the principal myths of Greece and Rome, and for its commentary on their origins and significance. With 64 illustrations by Michelangelo, Raphael, Titian, Rubens, Canova, Bernini and others. 480pp. 5⅜ x 8½. 0-486-27584-1

LIGHT AND SHADE: A Classic Approach to Three-Dimensional Drawing, Mrs. Mary P. Merrifield. Handy reference clearly demonstrates principles of light and shade by revealing effects of common daylight, sunshine, and candle or artificial light on geometrical solids. 13 plates. 64pp. 5⅜ x 8½. 0-486-44143-1

ASTROLOGY AND ASTRONOMY: A Pictorial Archive of Signs and Symbols, Ernst and Johanna Lehner. Treasure trove of stories, lore, and myth, accompanied by more than 300 rare illustrations of planets, the Milky Way, signs of the zodiac, comets, meteors, and other astronomical phenomena. 192pp. 8⅜ x 11. 0-486-43981-X

JEWELRY MAKING: Techniques for Metal, Tim McCreight. Easy-to-follow instructions and carefully executed illustrations describe tools and techniques, use of gems and enamels, wire inlay, casting, and other topics. 72 line illustrations and diagrams. 176pp. 8¼ x 10⅞. 0-486-44043-5

MAKING BIRDHOUSES: Easy and Advanced Projects, Gladstone Califf. Easy-to-follow instructions include diagrams for everything from a one-room house for bluebirds to a forty-two-room structure for purple martins. 56 plates; 4 figures. 80pp. 8¾ x 6⅜. 0-486-44183-0

LITTLE BOOK OF LOG CABINS: How to Build and Furnish Them, William S. Wicks. Handy how-to manual, with instructions and illustrations for building cabins in the Adirondack style, fireplaces, stairways, furniture, beamed ceilings, and more. 102 line drawings. 96pp. 8¾ x 6⅜. 0-486-44259-4

THE SEASONS OF AMERICA PAST, Eric Sloane. From "sugaring time" and strawberry picking to Indian summer and fall harvest, a whole year's activities described in charming prose and enhanced with 79 of the author's own illustrations. 160pp. 8¼ x 11. 0-486-44220-9

THE METROPOLIS OF TOMORROW, Hugh Ferriss. Generous, prophetic vision of the metropolis of the future, as perceived in 1929. Powerful illustrations of towering structures, wide avenues, and rooftop parks–all features in many of today's modern cities. 59 illustrations. 144pp. 8¼ x 11. 0-486-43727-2

THE PATH TO ROME, Hilaire Belloc. This 1902 memoir abounds in lively vignettes from a vanished time, recounting a pilgrimage on foot across the Alps and Apennines in order to "see all Europe which the Christian Faith has saved." 77 of the author's original line drawings complement his sparkling prose. 272pp. 5⅜ x 8½. 0-486-44001-X

THE HISTORY OF RASSELAS: Prince of Abissinia, Samuel Johnson. Distinguished English writer attacks eighteenth-century optimism and man's unrealistic estimates of what life has to offer. 112pp. 5⅜ x 8½. 0-486-44094-X

A VOYAGE TO ARCTURUS, David Lindsay. A brilliant flight of pure fancy, where wild creatures crowd the fantastic landscape and demented torturers dominate victims with their bizarre mental powers. 272pp. 5⅜ x 8½. 0-486-44198-9

Paperbound unless otherwise indicated. Available at your book dealer, online at **www.doverpublications.com**, or by writing to Dept. GI, Dover Publications, Inc., 31 East 2nd Street, Mineola, NY 11501. For current price information or for free catalogs (please indicate field of interest), write to Dover Publications or log on to **www.doverpublications.com** and see every Dover book in print. Dover publishes more than 500 books each year on science, elementary and advanced mathematics, biology, music, art, literary history, social sciences, and other areas.